ISBN 978-0-9573902-1-8
Published by Picture of Health Clubs (UK) Ltd.

PICTURE *of* **HEALTH** CLUBS®

Design and artwork: Steve Alport Art & Design.
Email: steve@alport-design.co.uk

ARE <u>YOU</u>
A PHYSICAL WRECK
OR
A MENTAL WASHOUT?
OR BOTH!

**The EASY way for YOU to achieve a FIT and STRESS-FREE life
no matter how busy you are**

by Lol Cohen
and Kev Murphy

Unwind body and mind...

Lol (Laurence) Cohen is the founder and guiding light of the Picture of Health Clubs. He was born and bred off Penny Lane, Liverpool and as a teenager frequented the Cavern Club whose acts turned Liverpool into the centre of the musical world. Surrounded by such musical legends it was only natural that he became an accountant!

As a Chartered Accountant Lol has spent his whole working life in business and accountancy. He really was that stressed man in chapter 1 and has suffered many misfortunes and personal tragedies in his life.

It was these events that made him re-assess his life and rebalance work and family. He has also spent most of his life doing Youth Work. His efforts and insights, combined with a study of the human physiology and stretching, has made him perfectly placed to promote the Picture of Health Clubs message to unwind body and mind.

Kev (Kevin) Murphy was born in Cardiff, Wales in the sixties when the space race and the lunar landings were front-page news. Kev believes that however many advances technology has made and the many answers it has given, science has never given a satisfactory answer of what it is to be human. This spurred him to study philosophy, religion and languages gaining a degree in philosophy and German. His thirst for knowledge continued as his study moved into other areas. It was during his study of Aikido as a means of self-awareness rather than just self-defence that convinced Kevin that one of the key areas of life is balance. His study of languages has led him to believe that humans are designed to communicate with each other and ourselves - something that we, in a media fuelled world, have lost sight of.

Kevin is a practical man. He believes that a truth, however profound, is useless if it cannot be easily applied to daily life. This belief was formed by his two decades doing his regular job, driving trains; a job he also did for the British Army part time in Germany. The balance of practical application with sound reasoning is one of the principles Kevin brings to the team.

The pair combined their different strengths and strategies to produce the Picture of Health Clubs unique balancing of body and mind.

In this ever-faster world with even more choice they believe the sanity of the Picture of Health Clubs message of *less is more*.

Contents

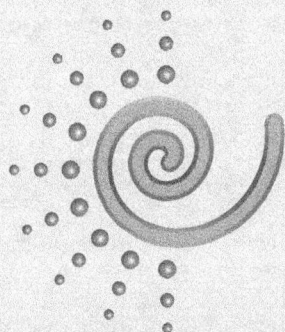

Unwind body and mind...

Welcome

Welcome to Picture of Health Clubs

This could be the first step to changing your life for the better.

We offer a unique philosophy that is a world away from traditional muscle-busting gyms or aerobic or exercise classes that go for 'the burn'. Our goals are easily summed up by our two mottos:

'*Unwind Body and Mind*'
And
'*Empower Body and Mind*'

What do we mean? – Read on and enter the world of Picture of Health.

THE DIFFERENCE

We at Picture of Health Clubs believe that for most of us to get FIT or stay FIT, both mentally and physically fit - we don't need to go to gyms or aerobic or dance classes. I'm not saying - don't go to them – if you go and enjoy them then that's great. But most people who take the plunge and join do not enjoy it, and the drop-out rate is huge. Health clubs make an awful lot of money from people who join, pay their signing up fees, pay their monthly subs – and don't go!

Madness!

Our belief is that for the majority of us, 'FIT' means:

- *Keeping our bodies as flexible as possible, especially as we get older.*
- *We have reasonably strong muscles.*
- *We can breathe without gasping for breath when we carry out a little extra work.*
- *We know how to relax – properly.*
- *We can keep our stress under control.*
- *We are able to take a positive attitude towards our lives.*

And finally:

- *Sensible but enjoyable eating.*

We will show you simple ways to achieve all of these objectives.

And what's more:

- *They will be easy to learn and do.*
- *You will enjoy them - honest!*
- *And you will be able to incorporate them into your daily lives – no matter how busy you may be.*

Specifically:

We will show you how to be FIT physically and mentally, easily and enjoyably.

We will show you how to balance your life to bring your stress levels under control.

We will help you to develop a feeling of Real Relaxation that will help you to unclutter your mind, so that you can think clearly. Thinking clearly will enable you to make better decisions in your life.

You will then find that you are developing this feeling of Real Relaxation into all your activities. Whether it's stretching, movement, walking, breathing, working, studying, what ever, you will become more focused and you will achieve more with less effort.

Sounds too good to be true – but it's fact.

What ever you are doing – you will work more efficiently and less stressfully.

And – as you develop you – will become more and more effective at taking a positive attitude to your life. Our powerful 'Positive Attitude' tools will empower you to combat and control the stressful situations that we all have to deal with from time to time, and help you to lead the life that You really want.

You will actually be able to take control!

In other words:

> *'Unwind Your Body and Your Mind'*
> And then
> *'Empower Your Body and Your Mind'*

Our simple message is:

Make small changes to your busy daily lives, develop the skills that we will show you and dramatically transform your life for the better.

You will be well on the path to becoming a Picture of Health.

Health Warning

This book is written in a light, chatty style. There is some humour and it is jargon-free and easy to read.

But do not confuse a light manner with a light message.

By cutting back on jargon we keep our message simple.
Some of the simplest things in life are the most powerful.

We are serious about the message we are giving you.

So, be careful – following the advice in our book could seriously improve your health.

How to Use This Book

With some books you start at the beginning and read through to the end. A novel is a good example of this.

With some other books you select bits that interest you; like a dictionary or a guide book.

This book is different again!

Part I is a mixture of a novel, an autobiography, and a bit of science (nothing scary!). So we would like you to read this part like a novel, from beginning to end. It's not very big, so do not worry.

After that you have a choice:

You can carry on reading through Part II. This consists of the reasons why life can get you down and what you can do to become a Picture of Health.

Or you can:

Browse through Part III before reading Part II. Part III is our 'Tool Box' of techniques and exercises. If you need a solution to a particular problem you will find it here.

To help you decide which part to read first here is a brief outline of the parts:

PART II

The How and the Why of the book has been deliberately stripped of technical, mystical and esoteric language that makes you reach for the dictionary. You may think that Part II is just a load of common sense because it is free from jargon. Well it is, and we will take that as a compliment. It has been deliberately written for the ordinary people; people like us, to understand. This is not 'dumbing down' but part of our philosophy of 'less is more'.

PART III

This is the Tool Box and as the name suggests it contains tools to fix the problems of your life. Like all tools they need someone to use them and a little practice before they are really effective. The tools are exercises, techniques, tricks, call them what you like. They are simple to learn and with practice they are very powerful ways to help you to become a Picture of Health. They are the 'What' of the book. What you can do to fix your problems.

And talking of problems you now have to decide how to continue reading. It's your choice and the book is designed to make that choice as personal as possible.

Need a quick fix to a problem? Find the tool in Part III to fix it.

Do you need reasons before doing things? You will find them in Part II.

Part of your life perfect? Well done. Ignore the relevant chapters!

Whatever you choose to do you will find the book of great help in becoming a Picture of Health.

So go on…turn the page!

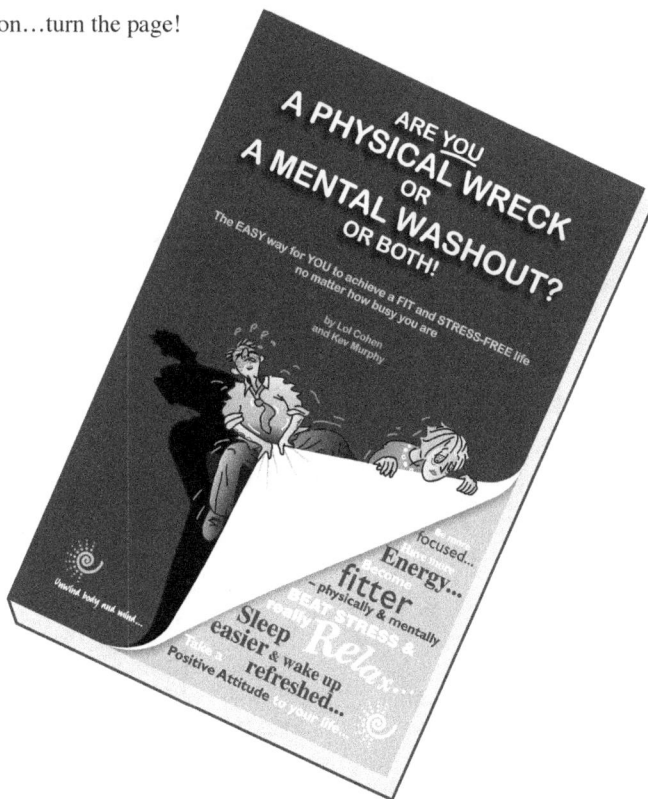

PART I

Chapter 1
My Former Life

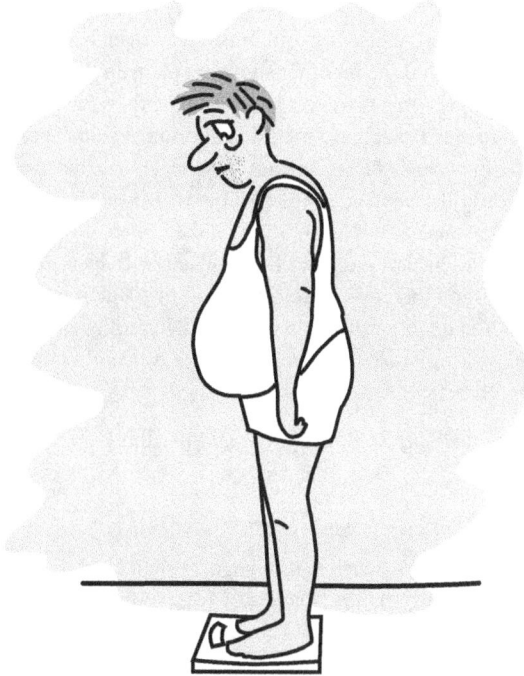

*'I always considered myself to be an 'ordinary' person – 'An average Joe'.
Then I thought – there is only one of me – so I must be unique.
If I'm unique - then I must be very special!*

*Never underestimate yourself. You are special. You can always do more than
you think'.*
L.C.

This book began on my 49th birthday. I looked down at my feet – and couldn't
see them – my belly blocked the view! So I looked back at my life, instead. I
told myself that I had reached an age where you start to look back rather than
forward.

I reviewed my life so far and came to the conclusion that I'd had a pretty raw deal. My life had had many ups and downs but I concluded that there had been many more downs than ups – in fact it had been pretty rough. The more I thought about it the worse it became. The more I analysed it the more I felt sorry for myself! The more that I felt sorry for myself the more depressed I became. By this time I was almost suicidal! What had I done to deserve such a raw deal?

So I began to look again at how I had analysed my life. I conceded that some of the events in my life were caused by circumstances over which I had no control whatsoever. I also accepted the fact that some events were through other people's mistakes. Maybe some events were just sheer bad luck – wrong time wrong place! But eventually I realised that most of the important events were down to me; caused by me alone, because of my attitude, my negativity, my stress, whatever! I started to see clearly the mistakes that I had made. How I should have been more positive about things and how I should have taken control of events rather than just reacted to them. On the one hand the realisation that most of my problems were caused by myself alone was a great shock to me. But at the same time it was like a revelation. It suddenly felt like a huge burden had been lifted from off my shoulders and I had a surge of wellbeing and felt a warm glow inside of me that I had not experienced before.

Still it is one thing realising something, it's another thing doing something about it!

How do you start? Where do you go? What do you do?

I used to do a bit of sport when I was younger – then it died away to nothing. I thought that it didn't really matter, because I was young and fit. I realised that I should do something and planned to – but never quite got round to it.

I wore many badges for my services to Stress. I was full of tension, stiff muscles, aches and pains, lack of mobility and lethargy. I had little energy and was totally unmotivated. In other words – totally stressed out and totally burned out.

Mind you it was not surprising, as I had experienced a very stressful life – full of many misfortunes and personal tragedies – more than most – so I had earned my badges!

Then at age 49 I couldn't see my feet and thought what a failure I was.

So I finally realised that I must do something before it was too late. I knew that I had to improve my physical and mental fitness. And I knew that somehow I had to take control of my stress. And I knew that I had to take control of my life.

But HOW?

The first thing I did was to check out gyms and various exercise classes, but I quickly decided that these were not for me. (I'll tell you a little later in this chapter why not.)

Next, I consulted my best friend, Jeff. 'Jeff, I'm overweight, full of stress, tension, stiff muscles, aches and pains, lack of mobility, lethargy, little energy and totally unmotivated. I feel as if my whole life has been one big failure. I haven't done any exercise for years – I'm 49 years old and I feel like an old man!' I've looked at gyms and exercise classes but I don't fancy them.'
'What should I do?'

'Why don't you do Aikido'
'What's Aikido?'
'It's a Japanese Martial Art which is a self-defence system using technique rather than strength. It will not only help you physically but mentally as well. It's ideal for people of all ages – even you!' (Reader's note – this is not a plug for Aikido – although I would recommend it to anyone)

It all sounded a bit too much for a failure like me – but in for a penny, in for a pound. I found a club near where I lived and started to go to classes.

I persevered with the classes and over a period of time my fitness started to improve, my outlook on life started to change and Aikido became my sport and my hobby. It wasn't easy for me – it was hard work and I suffered from many aches, pains, muscular strains and minor injuries. But I didn't give up – probably out of stubbornness!

As I pursued my new journey I began to wonder how on earth, by age 49, I had got myself into such a state.

Well - I don't have an A1 brain and I am not an academic. I'm just an 'Average Joe' an 'Ordinary Guy'. Still, I wanted to know what it was all about. So I began to do a bit of studying. I read articles in papers and magazines, and read many books. I also enrolled on various courses and actually ended up with a few more letters after my name. Nothing too special mind you – no PhDs, or MBAs; But I felt good because I had achieved something. I had a success – not bad for an ordinary person do I hear you say! And yes, I actually succeeded in attaining Black Belt status at Aikido.

I began to practise many of the things that I had learnt. I started to change my attitude to things and started to take control of my life.
Well, what a difference it has made!

The more that I read, studied and practised I began to realise that my life problems and my failures were not unique to me. Everyone at some time meets the same problems in life, many cope quite adequately with them but many, many more would appear not to.

It didn't take me long to come to the following conclusions:

FITNESS - EXERCISE

It goes without saying that everyone wants to stay fit and healthy. Most of us probably realise that we should be doing some exercise.

But – most of us don't - or we keep putting it off.

STRESS

Stress and stress-related illnesses are the number one health problem and the main reasons for time off work. Even in the comfort of our own homes, with all the labour-saving gadgets and the latest technology at our fingertips, families are trying to cope with levels of stress that were unheard of in generations gone by. Yet, a significant percentage of these people are unwilling or unable to seek help or take steps to help themselves to alleviate these problems.

We just live with it!

POSITIVE ATTITUDE

I looked around me and all I could see was miserable faces. So many people appeared to be miserable and so negative. There were certainly more 'frowners' than 'smilers'. I guess you could say that these are the people who always see a half empty glass rather than a half full glass. Don't these people realise that taking a positive attitude to their lives can transform their wellbeing and their potential?

Obviously not!

What chance – a healthy life, with some success and no stress.

We make all sorts of excuses to ourselves why we aren't doing something to help ourselves:

- Too busy.
- Haven't got the time.
- Don't need to yet.
- Etc. etc. etc!

Some of us may even have tried something.

After all there are loads of classes available – and gyms around every corner.

The trouble is – gyms tend not to be very inviting for most of us – with all their bits of High Tec. machinery – and all those sweaty individuals looking as if they will drop dead at any minute from their exertions.

Let's be honest, many of us have been to aerobic classes and dance/exercise classes – and found that we just can't keep up with the Lycra clad creatures that live there; and we finish the class feeling more stressed than when we started.

The other thing I noticed was that most of the participants were not enjoying themselves. It was as if they were enduring some prison sentence or torture, or taking some nasty medicine prescribed by their doctors. How sad!

There are also many other classes available. All the eastern disciplines, including the many Martial Arts, Tai Chi, Chi Gung, and the various forms of yoga. There are also all the other forms of western classes that come in and out of favour – whatever happens to be the latest 'fad' or 'the flavour of the month' at any particular time. These disciplines tend to require a high degree of dedication and perseverance because of their complexity. In order to progress you have to conform very much to 'their method' and most of us fall by the wayside. Even in my Aikido club, that is more 'user friendly' than most, we have a regular influx of new members, but few stay for very long.

Don't get me wrong – I'm not knocking any of these classes or disciplines. They do a fine job for those who are able to enjoy them. It's just that what they offer is not necessarily for us.

And

It would appear that 'US' is the majority of us. Despite the proliferation of gyms, Health Clubs and all sorts of other Sporting Facilities and relaxation classes of one sort or another, the percentage of the population NOT doing any EXERCISE, either mental or physical, on a regular basis is HUGE.

So I asked myself this question.

'What can be done to encourage this huge percentage of humanity to do something to help themselves?'

Well – I came to the conclusion that we need to do things that are:

- Easy to do.
- Moderate to do.
- Relaxing.
- Without pain.
- And things that we will enjoy.

ALSO – because we're such busy people it must be things that we can fit into our busy lives without difficulty.

AND finally – things that will quickly start to make us:

- Feel better.
- Feel healthier.
- Increase our energy levels.
- And, reduce our stress levels.

Before I tell you what I did, let me take you through a typical day before I changed my life for the better.

Chapter 2
My Old Typical Day

My alarm clock goes off with the sound of a steam ship's siren and frightens the living daylights out of me. With a flailing arm I hit the snooze button on the third attempt as I force one eye open to half focus on the clock it gives me its sad message – time to get up. I slump back onto the pillow with a curse convinced that I have only been in bed for twenty minutes. I've had another lousy night's sleep. Good morning world!

The alarm tries a second attempt to get me out of bed. I must be more awake now as I hit the snooze button first time. I now ponder the first problem of the day: 'Can I have another ten minutes in bed and still catch my train?' The answer is always 'Yes!' I return to my pillow content in the correctness of my calculations.

At the third attempt the alarm gets me out of bed – though this probably had more to do with the fullness of my bladder than the effectiveness of the alarm clock. I leap out of bed and in doing so strain my back. I swear as I shamble like a zombie to the bathroom – sweet relief. I fumble through my routines of washing and dressing and limp to the kitchen. My stomach now demands feeding but I have snoozed my breakfast time away. I sit nursing a cup of coffee instead. I check my work stuff as my coffee cools: bag, season ticket, keys,..Keys?..KEYS!?! Where the hell are they? I blame my partner, I blame the kids, I blame the keys. They should be on the key rack. I check the key rack, the draw, the table, the time – argh – late.

All logical systems of searching have been replaced by the 'Headless Chicken' approach. I check my bag, jacket pocket and the key rack again – still not there. I check the shelf, my coat – coat pocket. Got them! I look at myself in the hall mirror – how awful! I then grab the rest of my stuff and with a curse rush out of the house in a mad dash for the train. My caffeine breakfast now cold in the kitchen.

Why is it that when you are running late, trains are always on time? However those and other secrets of the universe must be solved later – my whole being is now focused on catching that accursed train. I just make it in a bath of sweat and grab a seat in the carriage. Achievement.

The stroll from the train station to work is short and I soon reach my office building. Then I notice the sign 'lift out of order.' It is a body blow. I look at the stairwell with the resignation of a condemned man. Five floors. I set off cursing the lift company, cursing the building managers, even cursing the promotion that gave me a fifth floor office six months ago.

I absolutely hate this forty-minute journey to work. I look around at my fellow commuters – all engrossed in their own private worlds – all pretending that they are not human beings. I see the same people looking at the same crossword, I pass the same houses, the same sheep? The MP3 player people with their tinny, hissing music and nodding their heads like exotic birds performing a mating dance. The book people sit engrossed in the latest novel. Some people even engage in conversation! I stare out of the window. It was interesting for the first year – watching the seasons change but now it is like a monotonous movie your children force you to watch over and over with them.

The stroll from the train station to work is short and I soon reach my office building. Then I notice the sign 'lift out of order.' It is a body blow. I look at the stairwell with the resignation of a condemned man. Five floors. I set off cursing the lift company, cursing the building managers, even cursing the promotion that gave me a fifth floor office six months ago. I finally arrive at the fifth floor reception and gasp an answer to my receptionist's greeting. My legs are like pieces of lead, my muscles have seized up and I can't catch my breath. I expect at any moment the first indications of a heart attack.

Against my own private fears I don't have a heart attack so I switch on the PC and begin work. After ten minutes my body reminds me that I missed breakfast. The solution: coffee and chocolate. A quick visit to the vending machine and the caffeine and calories work their magic. I feel full of energy and I tear through the rest of my work with ease.

It's 11.00am.and I am already starting to stiffen up – right on schedule. My body is starting to ache in all the usual places - legs, buttocks and lower back. My shoulders and neck muscles are, as usual, starting to tense up. My energy reserves have expired - need another coffee – urgently.

Later in the morning my deputy comes in: young, smartly dressed, confident and full of energy, I see an image of myself twenty years ago before the battering life has given me lowered my expectations, raised my stress levels and widened my waistline. I am secretly a little jealous of what I see.

> *Later in the morning my deputy comes in: young, smartly dressed, confident and full of energy, I see an image of myself twenty years ago before the battering life has given me lowered my expectations, raised my stress levels and widened my waistline. I am secretly a little jealous of what I see.*

My task is to evaluate my deputy's solution to a problem. I listen to the presentation and consider the solution. There are some good points in my deputy's report – some that I had not considered - but the conclusion is wrong and I waste no time in voicing this – loudly. My confrontational response receives an equally combative rebuttal. We both argue – I eventually win – after all I am the boss!

But did I really win? It doesn't seem like a victory. Did I get personal? The report did have some good points. The argument certainly didn't do any good for my stress levels and what about the ongoing relationship with my deputy? Best not think about it too much. Surely there's a better way?

My office clock and my stomach agree – it's lunchtime. I grab my coat and stride out of the office with thoughts of food filling my mind. Then a less pleasant thought enters my mind – the lift. The battle for food verses physical exhaustion and potential heart attack now occupies my mind until it is resolved by my receptionist: the lift is back in service. Praise be!

The local sandwich bar has its usual monumental choice of fillings: salad, tuna and mayo, chicken tikka. With the prospect of an afternoon ploughing through the Peterson report I opt for a bacon sandwich and a cola. I then return to the office to steal a half hour extra on the report. I hurry through the report's introduction and the bacon sandwich pausing only to note how bacon grease seems to get everywhere.

My opinion on the Peterson report is needed at 4 o'clock but my third reading of page 32 has given me the opinion that the report was written by a committee with only a passing acquaintance with English. It is just not making sense. I doggedly try again with no success. Is the report bad? Is it me? I look at the clock – half past two! One and a half hours to get a report typed. Grief! I have another feeling in my stomach – not hunger this time – panic. Quick – another coffee and an obligatory bar of chocolate.

Now I attempt the report again. Why can't they write in English? I check my notes, I check the time; is it getting hot in here? That knot in my stomach is getting tighter. Then suddenly enlightenment – I have got what they mean! I feverishly type my report. I print it off and then realise that I didn't use the spell checker. Spelling checked, second report printed and given to my secretary for forwarding to the ninth floor. And with ten minutes to spare!

The knot in my stomach begins to die away as does my energy. I blame it on running on adrenaline and the usual late afternoon energy slump. Only another hour and a half to go. A coffee will restore me. The last hour drags by and eventually five o'clock arrives. I squeeze into the lift with the rest of the weary workers.

> *At last I return to my home, which feels as if I left it in the previous ice age. I want five minutes peace but I am engulfed by the latest family squabble.*

The stroll to the station holds no special appeal as I wait with what seems the rest of humanity on the platform. Eventually the train arrives, only ten minutes late, and like cattle we squeeze into the coach.

I'm lucky I find a seat to collapse into. Normally I metaphorically collapse whilst standing up. I'm physically drained and mentally washed out. I don't remember the journey home – I never do. It's as if I'm on autopilot, using my own onboard satellite navigation system.

At last I return to my home, which feels as if I left it in the previous ice age. I want five minutes peace but I am engulfed by the latest family squabble.

With the threat of 'wait 'til your father gets home' my wife – the prosecutor - and the co-defendants – my ten-year-old boy and my teenage girl all talk together to get their point over. Suddenly I have to change from tired commuter to Moses the lawgiver. I try to listen to all three but in the end I lose my own temper and begin to shout louder than all the rest.

Eventually there is silence and with a feeling of dread I ask 'what's the problem?'

'She keeps picking on me 'cos I'm having burgers, dad.' Complains my boy whilst scowling at his sister.

'Meat is murder, dad!' retorts my teenage daughter.

I then remember her one girl campaign to turn the family, if not the world vegetarian. I hope this fad will be as short lived as the 'blue hair' phase.

'She's freaky, dad.' Returns my boy.

'No I'm not!'

'Yes you are.'

I look at my wife for support but none comes – she just shrugs her shoulders and returns to the kitchen to finish dinner. Facing the demonic duo alone I resort to the last refuge of a frustrated father – threats. I point at my teenager: 'Now young lady, don't pick on your brother or there will be no leather jacket for your birthday.' I take her sulky sigh as an agreement. I then turn to my young son, beaming with apparent victory. 'Stop calling your sister names or we'll feed you vegetarian food.' For my son, whose sole diet seems to read like the menu at Macdonald's this seems cruel and unusual punishment and he scampers off to the kitchen to ensure his burgers do not mysteriously turn into broccoli.

I slump in front of the television eating my dinner and watching the reality TV that takes my mind away from my own reality.

I slump in front of the television eating my dinner and watching the reality TV that takes my mind away from my own reality. Programmes include such topics as people buy house, people decorate house, people sell house, people locked in a house. After food the children remove themselves to their gadget-laden bedrooms to indulge themselves in more television or music and I find myself alone with my spouse worshipping the one-eyed god – the television. I sink into the couch as waves of tiredness wash over me.

I consider all the things that I was planning to do this evening. I consider them - and decide to put them off - again. I wallow in my couch. It seems to get more uncomfortable by the day. I know it's doing no good at all for my back. When it starts to ache I just try moving to a less painful position. That's the extent of my exercise tonight.

Eventually the clock agrees with my body that it is time to go to bed and I climb the stair with the alacrity of a condemned man climbing the scaffold. I collapse into bed but my mind does not want to switch off and countless thoughts fly through my head. I toss and turn, watch the clock, count sheep but I still seem to be as wide-awake as ever. I know that I will probably have a poor night's sleep as I still continue to worry about the day's problems.

Finally sleep overtakes...

Chapter 3
My New Typical Day

I wake just before the alarm goes off and hit the snooze button and slide back onto my pillow. As I come out of a good night's sleep I take a few moments to clear my mind and think of the day ahead. Now my mind is awake but my body is not so I gently start to stretch my body to life and go through my 'bedstretcher routine'. Slowly my body wakes up and I feel human again. It's amazing how this few minutes of physical and mental activity seems to set me up for the day.

The alarm sounds for a second time and this time I get out of bed turning the alarm off and head for the bathroom to wash and shower and then dress.

I ponder what to have for breakfast. Something simple: cereals and some orange juice if the kids have not drunk the lot. I check my work stuff as I finish the last of my juice: bag, season ticket, keys,..Keys?..KEYS!?! They should be on the key rack. Where the hell are they? I think for a moment: when did I last have them? Last night. Carrying heavy shopping, hands full, raining, coat on, in the coat pocket? Yes, got them!

As I leave the house I look at myself in the hall mirror and smile. I say to myself 'I'm going to have a good day!' I smile again.

> *As I leave the house I look at myself in the hall mirror and smile. I say to myself 'I'm going to have a good day!' I smile again.*

I stroll to the train station. Why is it that when you are on time trains are always late? However those and other secrets of the universe must be solved later as I grab a seat and settle down.

I used to absolutely hate this forty-minute journey to work but now I see it as an opportunity for actually doing something. What I actually do can vary from day to day but it's certainly better than wasting my time. I look around at my fellow commuters – all engrossed in their own private worlds – all pretending that they are not human beings. I see the same people looking at the same crossword, I pass the same houses, the same sheep? The MP3 player people with their tinny, hissing music and nodding their heads like exotic birds performing a mating dance. The book people sit engrossed in the latest novel. Some people even engage in conversation. I retrieve a small book from my bag – Spanish verbs for the next holiday.

The stroll from the train station to work is short and I soon reach my office building. I fail to notice the sign 'lift out of order.' I always take the stairs. I am not some sort of fit superman shunning all lifts but I decided to use the stairs after I got promotion to the fifth floor six months ago and noticing a few inches more waist than there was. I started slowly – first month I got off at the fourth floor, next month the third and so on. Now I manage all five without a problem.

I arrive at the fifth floor reception and answer to my receptionist's greeting. When I started using the stairs I could only gasp a reply - now I can talk.

I switch on the PC and begin work.

It's 11.00am so I get up from my desk and go through my little routines. I remember the old days when even by 11.00am I was so stiff and tense: wouldn't anyone who sits in the same position all day?

I have my midmorning coffee – lovely. I think to myself how much better I have been since I cut back on the coffee. Two, or sometimes three, each day is now fine. I sip at my glass of water. I always have a glass of water on the go. I remember when I thought it was tasteless!

It's 11.00am so I get up from my desk and go through my little routines. I remember the old days when even by 11.00am I was so stiff and tense: wouldn't anyone who sits in the same position all day?

Later in the morning my deputy comes to see me: young, smartly dressed, confident and full of energy, I see an image of myself twenty years ago. One of my tasks today is to evaluate my deputy's solution to a problem. I listen to the presentation and the solution and consider it. There are some good points in my deputy's report – some that I had not considered - but the conclusion is wrong.

I acknowledge the good points but state the conclusion is wrong. My deputy is a little crestfallen and says that perhaps I have not fully considered the report's points. I agree with the remark and ask my deputy to expand on them saying it is better to join heads than lock horns: it is not about winning the argument but getting a good solution. After a while we both come to a solution we are both happy with and my deputy feels encouraged rather than corrected.

Come midday and my office clock and my stomach agree – it's lunchtime. I grab my coat and stride out of the office with thoughts of food filling my mind. The local sandwich bar has its usual monumental choice of fillings: salad, tuna and mayo, chicken tikka. With the prospect of an afternoon ploughing through the Peterson report I opt for a bacon sandwich and a mineral water. Rather than returning to the office to steal a half-hour extra on the report I head for the park and a half-hour away from the office to clear my mind.

My opinion on the Peterson report is needed at 4 o'clock but my third reading of page 32 has given me the opinion that the report was written by a committee with only a passing acquaintance with the English language. It is just not making sense. I doggedly try again with no success. Is the report bad? Is it me? I look at the clock – half past two. One and a half hours to get a report typed. Grief! I have another feeling in my stomach – not hunger this time – panic. I attempt the page again. There are only four pages after that for goodness sake. Why can I not make head or tail of this? I cast the report onto my desk in disgust. A solution is needed – am I stressed? I think 'stress check'. I get up from my desk and go through one of my little workouts and I take a sip from my glass of water.

I return to my desk and the report now with a clear mind for another attempt. Why can't they write in English? Then suddenly enlightenment – I have got what they mean! I triumphantly type my report. After I have printed it off I realise that I did not use the spell checker. Spelling checked and a second report is printed and given to my secretary for forwarding to the ninth floor. And with time to spare.

With the report disappearing to the ninth floor so my energy disappears. I blame it on running on adrenaline and the usual late afternoon energy slump – only another hour and a half to go. The second coffee of the day will restore me and my last of the day as I begin the caffeine curfew that ensures a good night's sleep. The last hour drags by but eventually five o'clock comes and I head for the stairs avoiding the squeeze into the lift with the rest of the weary workers; it's easier going down stairs. The stroll to the station holds no special appeal as I wait with what seems the rest of humanity on the platform. Eventually the train arrives, only ten minutes late, and like cattle I squeeze into the coach. I am lucky, I find a seat.

At last I return to my home, which feels as if I left it in the previous ice age. I want five minutes peace but I am engulfed by the latest family squabble.

With the threat of 'wait 'til your father gets home' my wife – the prosecutor - and the co-defendants – my ten-year-old boy and my teenage girl all talk together to get their point over. Suddenly I have to change from tired commuter to Moses the lawgiver. I try to listen to all three but in the end I say that I will change and be happy to listen to them in five minutes. I use the five minutes wisely and as I change my clothes I use the opportunity to clear my head and unwind from 'work mode'. One of my little workouts is ideal.

I've now changed out of my suit and feel more 'dad-like' in casual clothes though I think that perhaps a judge's wig and robe would be better for this occasion. When I return there is silence and with a feeling of dread I ask 'what's the problem?'

'She keeps picking on me 'cos I'm having burgers, dad.' Complains my boy whilst scowling at his sister.

'Meat is murder, dad!' retorts my teenage daughter.

I then remember her one girl campaign to turn the family, if not the world vegetarian. I hope this fad will be as short lived as the 'blue hair' phase.

'She's freaky, dad.' Returns my boy.

'No I'm not!'

'Yes you are.'

I look at my wife for support but none comes – she just shrugs her shoulders and returns to the kitchen to finish dinner.

Facing the demonic duo alone I resort to the last refuge of a frustrated father – confuse them. I address my teenager: 'Now young lady, how can you call meat murder and still want a leather jacket for your birthday?' She looks confused as she has to decide one fashion from another. I take her sulky sigh as an agreement to a temporary peace. I then turn to my young son, beaming with apparent victory. 'You call your sister freaky yet have you eaten vegetarian food? Perhaps we should all try it for a few months. Might do us all good.' For my son, whose sole diet seems to read like the menu at Macdonald's this seems cruel and unusual punishment and he scampers off to the kitchen to ensure his burgers do not mysteriously turn into broccoli.

I enjoy my evening meal and then review my activities for the evening. What is it tonight? I have a varied list of evening activities. Sometimes I have to do some work for my job, but not tonight. Other activities might include socialising with friends or relations, a visit to the pub for a quick one, some reading or listening to music. Most nights I try to go for a 'brisk' 20 to 30 minutes walk. I sometimes take the wife along - walking hand in hand is like we are both courting again. It's amazing how regular walking really feels good.

OK - after a walk with the wife we both settle down to watch my favourite TV programme. The children have removed themselves to their gadget-laden bedrooms to indulge themselves in whatever kids of their age do. I sink into the couch and get really relaxed and comfortable. I consider what a wise investment it had been to change my couch. The old one seemed comfortable but it was killing my back.

Eventually the clock agrees with my body that it is time to go to bed. I climb the stairs thinking to myself that for a working day it hasn't been too bad. I relax into bed and end my day with one of the various routines that I have been working on. I say to my wife 'Pleasant dreams'.

Sleep soon overtakes me...

Chapter 4
Fitness

'The first time I see a jogger smiling, I'll consider it'.
Joan Rivers

WHY EXERCISE?

You only have to mention the word 'Exercise' and what happens?

People go weak at the knees. People shudder and go pale. People start to sweat and disappear.

And that's before they exercise!

But – what does 'exercise' really mean?

We say it means:

Using your body and your mind - to do a little extra each day to keep you fit. Being FIT is one of the ways to get the best out of life. I think we all can relate to that. The arguments start when we try to define fitness.

The army produces a definition of fitness for our fighting men. They need to be fit to survive the rigours of the battlefield. But almost all frontline soldiers retire before they get to 40. Let's be honest about it – we all want to be fit - whatever our age.

Another definition is an absence of disease, injury and a lengthened lifespan. That is certainly a goal but it is a bit of a loose definition.

One fact is definite – everyone in the 'civilised' world is living much longer than his or her forebears. The medical profession is producing more and more pills and potions to prevent or save us from life threatening diseases and illnesses.   The average life expectancy is now well past the Bible's three score and ten. Where will it end? Will we eventually live for hundreds of years? Who can say?

However, one thing is definite. There is no point living longer unless you are going to enjoy a decent quality of life.

And in order to enjoy a decent quality of life you need to be FIT – that is – Picture of Health Clubs FIT.

Age does not come into it. Even if you are over 40 then you can still qualify! In fact it doesn't matter what age you are – YOU QUALIFY.

Our Picture of Health Clubs definition of fitness is not just that we are physically fit:

It is being FIT in body and mind.

So let's break down our definition a little bit further:

- *Flexibility* – Your body can twist, turn and bend easily.

- *Good strength* – Your muscles are reasonably strong. For example, you can get up out of a low chair easily (See the OOH-AAH test at the end of this page). You can walk up and down stairs without aching all over. You can carry reasonably heavy bags etc. without strain.

- *Breathing endurance* – You can walk or run reasonable distances without gasping for breath. I mean running for the bus not a marathon!

- *Relaxing* – Be able to really relax and do things with a relaxed body and mind.

- *Stress* – You are able to keep stress well under control.

- *Positive Attitude* – You are able to take a positive attitude towards your life.

And finally –

- *Food* – Sensible but enjoyable eating.

Do you fail the OOH-AAH Test?

How many of you fail the OOH-AAH test?

Probably those of you who have reached such a state of physical deterioration (stiffness) that getting in and out of chairs and settees becomes a major effort.

You do know the OOH-AAH test:
You are sitting in your chair or settee and you want to stand up. So you grab the arms or seat, force yourself up as you go OOH!

And then when you go to sit down, you drop down ever so carefully, using your arms as levers as you go AAH!

Sad isn't it?................and you're only how old?

Well it shouldn't be like that........even at your age!

'Well' some of you might say, 'if that's all there is to your definition of fitness, what is the problem?'

Well, the trouble is that so many of us have this perception that in order to get fit we will have to exercise (mentally or physically – or both) really hard, often, and for a long time.

And

In order for the exercise to work we are going to suffer (feel pain).

You've heard the phrase 'No Pain – No Gain'.

Basically – that's all a load of rubbish.

If you want to become an Olympic athlete you will have to work very hard for a long time and suffer. If this is your aim, that's fantastic. Can we suggest that you will find some really useful stuff in this book to help you – but the physical bits go a bit beyond our expertise.
Seek professional coaching help elsewhere.

We encourage fitness for ordinary people – busy people who would like to get the benefits of fitness in their lives without having to live in the gym. We do encourage exercise but as you read on you will see that we have made them as simple and as user friendly as possible.

Even the busiest of people will be able to select some of the many options to fit into their ever so busy lives.

Let's look at some of the reasoning behind our definition of Fitness:

WHY BE FLEXIBLE?

When we were young we took fitness, flexibility and movement for granted. Look at any group of kids playing – they have boundless energy – and are able to contort their bodies into all sorts of physical movements, without any effort or discomfort what so ever.

Look at us now!

Stiff, lack of flexibility, back pain, headaches, depression, tiredness, lethargy, stressed out, etc. etc. etc.
Yet so many of us think that these symptoms are normal – just part of adulthood.

Actually, so much of it is due to the modern lifestyles that we lead. Motor vehicles and the continuing proliferation of labour saving devices enable us to constantly reduce, more and more, the extent of our physical exertions. It seems to us that in the not too distant future you will be able to sit in your big armchair in front of your big TV and do all your daily activities by using a remote control device held in your hand.

And they call that progress.

Then as we get older we become more and more stiff and less mobile. You would be amazed at the percentage of not so old people who cannot even get up and down stairs, or in and out of a settee without some assistance. (Try the OOH-AAH Test again).

But it doesn't have to be like this – and it doesn't have to mean regular visits to the gym, or aerobic, exercise or dance classes.

Our bodies have a tremendous capacity for movement and flexibility but if we don't regularly use our muscles they will eventually forget how to work. Then – other muscles have to compensate to enable us to move – and so the downward spiral towards immobility grows apace.

The statement 'Use it or lose it' definitely applies to muscles.

AND – THE GOOD NEWS IS:
A regular relaxing stretching routine will make a major contribution to fitness.

For some reason stretching is now the preserve of professional athletes and cats. Yet a good stretch, well performed, can boost health. Look at the advantages:

- You can blend it into your daily life – easily.
- It is not time consuming.
- You don't need special clothing or equipment.
- It is not painful to do.
- It is slow and relaxing.
- Everyone can do it regardless of age, degree of flexibility or level of fitness.

AND THE RESULTS:

- Will make you more flexible and less prone to injury.
- Will improve the way you feel.
- Will enable you to do that work/exercise at the weekend without aching backs, strained or pulled muscles etc.
- Will increase your energy levels.
- Will reduce your stress levels.
- Will reduce the tensions in your body.
- Will help to clear your mind and think clearly.

See the Tool Box 'WHY STRETCH? AND HOW!'

WHY GOOD STRENGTH?

Hopefully you now agree that having flexible muscles is a good idea. So don't you think that it would also be a good idea that our muscles are also reasonably strong?
Now, we're not talking about Mr Weightlifter filling himself full of steroids. We're not even suggesting that you need to go to a gym and pump iron. All we are saying is that the average person (most of us) should have muscles that are strong enough to easily cope with normal every day tasks.
These tasks will include walking up and down stairs, carrying reasonably heavy loads like your shopping bags – and yes – getting in and out of chairs and settees without going OOH-AAH!

See the Tool Box. 'The Strength Tool' will guide you in a weight-free, low impact workout.

WHY BREATHE?

A silly question perhaps, but such an important point that we have devoted a whole chapter to it in The Tool Box together with a Breathing Tool to help you breathe better.

Intrigued? Well, don't hold your breath waiting to get to them. *Turn to The Tool Box and look up 'Why Breathe? And How!' and 'The Breathing Tool'.*

The last four items in our definition of fitness are:

- *Relaxing.*
- *Stress.*
- *Positive Attitude.*
- *Sensible but enjoyable eating.*

The next few chapters cover these very important items.

Before you turn to the next page read this:

Our definition of fitness is one of balance. Those people not chasing specific fitness goals, like athletes etc, do not need to spend hours training. We are looking for a strong, flexible and healthy body carrying a relaxed and unstressed mind. We focus on economy of movement, breathing, and life. In other words we aim to do less and achieve more.

> **The Picture of Health Clubs definition of FIT**
>
> *Flexibility.*
>
> *Reasonably strong.*
>
> *Reasonable breathing endurance.*
>
> *Able to relax.*
>
> *Control stress.*
>
> *Positive attitude.*
>
> *Sensible eating.*

Less = More.

As you progress through the book you will see there is a constant theme to this mysterious 'Less = More'. All will be revealed in due course.

Read on and become a Picture of Health!

Chapter 5
Relaxing

The key component in achieving a fit and stress-free lifestyle

'How beautiful it is to do nothing, and then to rest afterwards'.
Spanish proverb

We have all heard the proverb 'All work and no play makes Jack a dull boy.' Well, that proverb is almost right; it is not play that we need to replace work, but relaxation. So how exactly do we relax?

I was at a party a while ago and asked the people there what they considered to be a relaxing time. Here are a few of the answers that I got:

- *Good music, good wine and a good book.*
- *Golf.*
- *No kids.*
- *A walk over the mountains.*
- *The garden.*
- *A few beers in the pub with the lads.*

Pretty much the answers you would expect from people. But these activities are relaxing in nature only because they are different from your work – in other words 'play'. But when you play you are still doing something, and in the 'doing' your focus shifts from relaxing to achieving. Let's re-visit the list I got from the party and emphasise what they want to achieve:

- *Listen to good music, enjoy good wine and read a good book.*

- *Play a round of golf in the minimum of strokes.*

- *Achieve something without worrying about keeping the kids occupied, clean, dry, fed, watered, apart whilst fighting, together whilst shopping, warm, or cool, out of the road, out of the cupboard, with their favourite toy, without wrecking the shop display, etc, etc.*

- *Climbing the mountain.*

- *Cultivating the garden.*

- *Keeping up with the lads in the pub.*

Rephrased like this these activities can sound like exchanging one hell for another; especially if you do not like roaming over mountains or digging the garden.

Even if you find doing all of the above relaxing it is not REAL relaxation, as you are still doing something – however relaxed you think it makes you.

I was 'stressed out' for years and really suffered both physically and mentally. I tried all the above diversions and more to take my mind away from the stress of my life. I signed up to the lie that a change is as good as a rest and it made matters worse. After all you do not run a marathon then go weight training in the hope that changing your exercise would rest your body.

No, you have to rest your mind and your body – i.e. you relax! I eventually understood the importance of 'learning to relax' and I intend to share it with you.

So what do I mean by relaxation? Real Relaxation is simply just not worrying about anything or doing anything. Now I do not mean being asleep! Rather it is a technique, a trick if you like, which completely relaxes your body and clears your mind enough to face the next round of life.

Our definition of Real Relaxation is:

- *Doing nothing – physically and mentally.*

- *Simply allowing your mind and your body to find a natural and calm state.*

- *Allowing your conscious mind to clear itself from all your daily stresses, feelings and thoughts.*

- *Allowing all the muscles of your body to relax and enabling all the areas of tension in your body to dissipate.*

- *Easy natural breathing.*

As you develop Real Relaxation you will start to feel the following benefits in your everyday life:

- *A body that has strong yet relaxed muscles, and joints that are free of stiffness that enable you to enjoy a full range of movement.*

- *Relaxed and easy breathing.*

- *A clear, calm and alert mind.*

In other words you will feel physically and mentally relaxed. Real Relaxation will enable you to let go of stress, your anxiety and your muscle tension.

Real Relaxation will enable you to:

- *Be more positive and focused.*
- *Think more clearly.*
- *Accomplish more.*
- *Improve personal relationships.*
- *Enjoy life more.*

It will:

- *Lower blood pressure.*
- *Improve circulation.*
- *Raise energy levels.*
- *Enable your body's systems to work more efficiently.*
- *And dramatically reduce your stress levels.*

You might be saying to yourself 'this all sounds too good to be true – and even if it is true it's going to cost a lot of time and effort'.

Well it is true that like most things in life, there is a cost, however...

First the truth:

Real Relaxation will give you all the above benefits. Do not just take our word for it: plenty of books and articles have been written to support our claim. The findings are the same; it is just that the Picture of Health Clubs way is different. We will show you simple techniques to follow that you can incorporate into your busy lifestyles virtually anywhere – and from the minute you start practising them you will start to feel benefits.

Now the cost, but it's only a little cost – more of an investment really.

Like everything in life, the more that you practise something the better you will become at it. So it is with RR (Real Relaxation), the more you do it the sooner you will enjoy all the benefits to which we refer.

Now if you think it a bit strange that you have to practice doing nothing you would not be alone. But the Picture of Health RR includes body and mind. Remember one of the aims of RR? Allowing your conscious mind to clear itself from all your daily stresses, feelings and thoughts. With all of life buzzing about your brain, believe me, getting a clear mind can take some practice!

> *Allowing your conscious mind to clear itself from all your daily stresses, feelings and thoughts. With all of life buzzing about your brain, believe me, getting a clear mind can take some practice.*

Having read all this so far some of you might be thinking about the 'M' word.

The 'M' word?

Meditation

When meditation enters into a subject many people find it all a bit 'freaky'. We would prefer not to mention the 'M' word for this reason but if we did not, many of you would say – why not? So let's have a common sense Picture of Health Clubs look at Meditation and try to de-bunk some myths.

What happens when people hear the word 'Meditation'?

If they are old enough they may remember the 60s and the Maharishi, the Beatles, Hari Krishna and Transcendental Meditation (TM). Others will imagine Yogis wrapped only in loincloths sitting on some lonely mountain top in Tibet, deep in some state of trance. Others may say it's just some eastern Mumbo Jumbo that involves beads and sandals.

It's no wonder we call it the 'M' word when we talk in public!

But, what is it really and what does it do?

Meditation is an altered state of consciousness achieved at will (i.e. without drugs) through physical and mental relaxation. Some people achieve this by concentrating on a single thing. Secular (non-religious) or religious contemplation and prayer can also achieve it.

The science bit is that your brain slows down and your brainwaves (the electrical impulses that are constantly flowing around your grey matter) slow down. They start to change from normal quick beta waves to the slower alpha and theta waves.

Meditation has been a common part of many eastern religions and their way of life for many thousands of years and is widely understood by those people. In the western world meditation was something that was only really understood by certain religious folk and philosophers. As the west became more secular so the general population lost touch with it.

Meditation only started to become more known again in the west when interest in all things eastern started to develop round about the 1960s. Today, it is very common. Many different organisations and groups and medical practitioners encourage people to meditate for many different reasons. The benefits are very similar to those we have described for Real Relaxation.

The trouble is so many people don't understand it and just can't do it. They just get totally screwed up with it. They're waiting for something to happen and for most it doesn't. Maybe it's because the average westerner has been brought up in an environment where all forms of contemplation and inward looking is no longer part of our culture. So what happens?

They try.
They pretend.
They stop.

You might ask 'What's the difference between your Real Relaxation and Meditation?'

Well the answer is that with Real Relaxation we are not seeking enlightenment. Nor are we seeking any altered states of consciousness - unless you count the change from stress to relaxed. We are simply training our body and mind as described in our definition.

If you actually achieve an altered state of consciousness – meditation – then fantastic, you are one of the lucky ones.

But for most of us – how would we know?

We certainly don't plug ourselves into a machine that measures our brainwave patterns when we practise our Real Relaxation.

Real Relaxation will give you all the benefits that we have described without any of the hang-ups, or wearing beads!

Taking time out to relax is a great way to face the next task. But do not think that we believe life should be a continuous cycle of stressful activity followed by a period of Zen-like calm before the next dose of stress. Real Relaxation is much more subtle.

Remember how we warned you about the need to practise Real Relaxation? As you will soon find, if you have not tried it already, when you try to empty your mind the world tries to break in. You may be alone; the surroundings may breathe serenity and tranquillity. You empty your mind...then suddenly the world breaks in: the gutters need fixing, Aunt Maggie's birthday, the vet's bill. Your peace is shattered.

Yet with practice it will become easier and easier to keep those daily worries out of your calm mind and gain some Real Relaxation. But that's not all. The more that you develop your Real Relaxation you will start to find that just as the world was breaking in to your calm mind so your calm mind will start to affect your daily activities. We call this Active Relaxation.

ACTIVE RELAXATION

This is where it gets really interesting. So far we have been going on about Real Relaxation and doing nothing. This is a powerful tool to rid yourself of stress. Yet most of us need to do something to put food on the table. And when we do something our relaxed mind slips away and stress returns.

The more you practice Real Relaxation you more you will find that the relaxation of body and mind is filtering into all your daily work and recreational activities. Whatever you are doing, you will start to feel more alive and alert, yet relaxed. You will become aware that unwanted physical and mental tensions have been eliminated.

Your mind will be much clearer and you will become far more aware and sensitive to yourself, to others, your surroundings and the job in hand.

You will be working more efficiently and less stressfully.

You will start to realise that everything becomes less of an effort.

You will actually be achieving MORE by doing LESS!

LESS MEANS MORE?

We live in a culture that lays great emphasis on hard work. 'The more effort that you put in to a project, the more that you will get out of it' is a typical statement. However 'effort' is often misunderstood. To perform an action more efficiently, one must generally do less – and actually learn how to not make an effort. As you become more able to relax the muscles of your body and your mind when you perform any task, the more you will achieve. Relaxation is the key to speed, quicker reaction times and efficiency.

Just watch professional dancers at work: effortless movement because they are relaxed. Anybody who is an athlete, dancer or who practises Aikido or many other martial arts will understand exactly what I am saying.

> *Learning to use only as much effort as is necessary is an important way of developing optimum health and vitality and it is an important ingredient in controlling stress.*

Obviously when I say 'relaxed' I don't mean so relaxed that you will fall over or go to sleep. I mean being physically and mentally relaxed but still totally 'switched on'. Real Relaxation will help you to achieve all this.

As you develop your relaxation skill you will soon realise that:
Less Effort = More Gain

Learning to use only as much effort as is necessary is an important way of developing optimum health and vitality and it is an important ingredient in controlling stress.

RELAXATION IS A SKILL

Relaxation is a skill and as with any other skill some people are born naturals - and then there are the rest of us. Fortunately any of us can acquire this skill.

And it doesn't require us to attend college for three years or go on lots of courses.

All you need to do to develop this skill and transform your life is to start incorporating some of the Tool Box workouts into your daily life.

Remember, it doesn't matter how busy you are – you will have the time for the workouts – and then guess what – you will find that you have more time available.

And with all skills, practice makes perfect.

Putting You in the Picture

Real Relaxation is:

- *Doing nothing – physically and mentally.*

- *The key component to a fit & stress-free lifestyle.*

Active Relaxation is:

- *Efficient moving and thinking.*

- *Achieving MORE by doing LESS.*

Chapter 6
Stress

Look after the pennies..... an alternative view

'Stress is not what happens to us. It's our response TO what happens.
And RESPONSE is something we can choose'.
Maureen Killoran

None of us go through life without encountering stress. In fact stress is one of the things that define us as human: from the time man began to walk upright, he ran upright, and away from sabre-toothed tigers, bears and other cavemen.

Things are a lot less dangerous now but a lot more stressful. We may not be chased by 400 lb. of teeth and claws but stress can be just as deadly; and we do not benefit from that adrenaline boost that prehistoric carnivores can produce - or the fitness benefits of all that running away.

So being human means meeting stress. Let's look at the big stress making moments of life. Some may happen to you, some may not. However, I can promise you that you will probably experience at least one of the following:

Big Stress Makers

- *The death of a parent.*
- *Redundancy.*
- *Divorce.*
- *Loss of a loved one.*
- *Illness.*
- *Moving house.*
- *Retirement.*

These are BIG stress makers. Perhaps the biggest. But they are part of life. And here is where my view of stress may be a little unorthodox. These stress-makers may be big, even life changing, but they are not the worst makers of stress in people's lives. In the great scheme of things some of these events may be tragic but just like the caveman running from his tiger, we humans are designed to deal with big stresses in life.

You may be disagreeing with me now. 'I'm not designed to deal with big stress.' I hear you say. Well read on – I hope to convince you.

If you suffer from one of the above how would you feel? Angry? Sad? Guilty? At a loss? Possibly all of them.

But, in big times of stress what happens? Families and friends rally round. You can expect help and support from your church, your work, your doctor, the job centre, etc. People expect you to be down; they want you to let it all out. Tears, anger, whatever you need to get over it – it has been a shock for you. You are given time and means to deal with your stress. Good.

This stress will hit you like a giant wave. But if you are strong – and most of us are – the wave will wash over you. Rather like a giant wave hitting a rock on a beach – the wave may move the rock but it will remain whole.

Little Stress Makers

That big rock can handle the big wave but a tiny stream of water will wear away that rock over time. I believe that it is the tiny stresses of life that wear us out just like the rock that is slowly worn by the water. The little stresses seem like nothing, and on their own, for a short period, they are. But over time they will wear you away and when they do, this time you are on our own. Our friends and relatives, our doctor and work colleagues do not bother to assist us with such trivial things.

You hear 'get over it – it is nothing!' and 'you must rise above it!' And like a man treading water you can for a while – maybe a long while – but eventually if you do nothing about it - you will drown.

Look what finally makes a person crack – it is not usually one of the big things that push him over the edge, rather it is something that is seemingly trivial – the car does not start, you lose your wallet, you have mislaid something in the house. Not a big creator of stress, but it is the straw that broke the camel's back.

THE STRESS INDUSTRY

We see stress everywhere: at work, at home, on the TV, on the radio, in newspapers, magazines and books.

Stress is big business. There is a whole industry out there that measures, advises and tries to cure stress. Thousands of people are earning a living helping the stressed, from psychiatrists dealing with clinical depression to lifestyle gurus who tell you where to put your houseplant.

Stress counsellors, psychologists, shrinks etc. are in such demand that – guess what – they're stressed out trying to cope with the demand for their services.

> *Stress is THE disease of the 21st century.*

Stress is THE disease of the 21st century. We are told all the time that stress is out there stalking us like the grim reaper. Magazine and newspaper articles tell us of the new way to combat stress. Radio programmes continually tells us to relax. TV shows us heart-rending stories about people who have endured stressful events in their life. Stress seems to be closing in on us!

One article I read on stress claimed that it is indeed the 21st century disease and that we did not suffer from it in the past and in the future the doctors will wonder what all the fuss was about. Well one thing is for sure, stress does exist now – ask anyone who suffers from it. But remember the stress industry has a vested interest in maintaining the fear and profile of stress.

After all if I were to create a pill that cured stress once and for all then a lot of counsellors, lifestyle gurus and authors of self-help books would be out of a job. But at least I would not feel stressed about it.

STRESS MYTHS

There are quite a few myths about stress that have gained currency over the years and really need to be de-bunked. Let's look at them: -

MYTH 1 – ALL STRESS IS BAD

Nonsense. Too much stress is bad for you but some stress can spur you on to do things. Many people in high-flying jobs actually enjoy a bit of stress to give them that adrenaline buzz to achieve. For mere mortals the annoying stresses of life – the little things that make you go 'oh bother' (or something stronger) – these frustrations of life can spur you on to create a solution. If it was not for generations of people going 'oh bother' and applying their mind to a problem then most of the things that make life a little easier would not have been invented!

MYTH 2 – LIFE WAS LESS STRESSFUL FOR OUR PARENTS

Rubbish. Everything looks better at a distance. Remember the grass is always greener on the other fellow's grave! Certainly things were different – was job security better when employers had more power to sack you at a whim? Most people rented their homes so there was no worry about mortgage payments – just the rent. My parents lived at a time when the world was at war. What would you rather face? Finding monthly payments or dodging nightly bombing raids? I know what I would find more stressful.

MYTH 3 – THE PACE OF LIFE IS GETTING FASTER

What? Is the world spinning faster? Are there only 22 hours in the day now? If anything the pace of life is getting slower for we have more spare time. Yet rather than using this time to relax and recharge our batteries we appear to fill our lives with all sorts of other things. If you really want to see what the pace of life was like a hundred years ago then do not use all the labour-saving devices that have been created over the last century. Walk to the shops (no car), and every day (no fridge). Hand-wash everything and dustpan and brush rather than use a vacuum cleaner. Do not worry about having a TV to relax in front of – you will be too exhausted to watch it.

DEALING WITH STRESS

Going back to big stress verses little stress, let us look at two examples:
Big stress. The death of a spouse.
Little stress. You have a boss who makes your life hell in work.

With the big stress there is nothing you can do to bring your spouse back to life. No amount of anger, grief or tears will bring him or her back. The situation is beyond your control. There is nothing you can do about it. All you can do is get on with your life as best as you can. People understand this and give you time and support. The mountain of grief seems insurmountable but in time you will get over it.

With the little stress – your boss makes your life hell. So, what are you going to do about it? That short question is the whole point of my argument about little stress and why it is so deadly.

With little stresses you have the stress coming at you from both directions: the cause of the stress – in this example your boss; and the other direction – the fact that you could, and therefore probably should do something about it. Double the stress!

Because the solution to your stress is within your control people are less supportive and you feel that you are on your own. This magnifies the stress even more. That is why the second stress myth – that things were less stressful for our parents - has gained currency. When the bombs were dropping on my parents from the sky everybody was in the same boat – or should I say air-raid shelter. When you have to find the next mortgage payment – you are on your own.

Whilst the big stress will eventually be overcome with time, the little stresses tend to grow until they overwhelm you.

THE SOLUTION

So what is the solution to the small but deadly stresses of life?

The first thing we must do is to short circuit our natural reaction to stress. For most of the history of humanity the reaction to stress has been action (fight or flight) rather than a reasoned response and it has served us well. For example:

Stress (tiger) = action (run) = result (escape)
Rather than
Stress (tiger) = reasoned response (think about it) = result (tiger food)

But a reasoned response is what is needed do deal with the little stresses of life where an impulsive action could be the worst thing to do. Look at these examples:

STRESS	IMPULSIVE ACTION	REASONED RESPONSE
I hate my job.	I quit!	Get a transfer or a New job.
My partner is Always grumpy.	Dump him!	Find out the cause by talking.
Money is short.	Sell the house!	Make a budget.

WHAT'S THE ANSWER?

Unfortunately I cannot give you the answer to your problem small stresses. Maybe dumping your grumpy boyfriend is the right choice. I don't know what will be the best solution for you – it's your life, you know the particular circumstances surrounding your stress and ultimately you must make the decision. You can and should seek appropriate advice but ultimately you must make a decision.

AAAH! More stress. I have to make a decision.

I'm afraid so.

But – the trouble is that you cannot make a good decision whilst you are stressed.

To make a reasoned choice and come to a good decision you have to be calm and have a clear mind.

And how do you get calm and have a clear mind?

The Answer

The answer is in two parts:

1. Firstly you must short circuit your natural reaction to impulsive action or reaction to a stressful event and give yourself time to come up with a reasoned response. Please refer to the Tool Box – 'Don't Panic!' tool. This simple four point plan will provide you with a simple method to combat your natural emotive reaction to stress.

2. Now you have time to calm and clear your mind. With a clear mind you are better able to consider the alternatives to your situation, seek appropriate advice if necessary, and then be able to make a genuine considered decision. Develop your clear mind by practising the 'Mind Focus' tool. Reinforce this tool when you are ready by practising 'Mind Power' tools, 'The Writing' tools and 'Inner Smile' tool.

I hope that you can now appreciate the importance of learning how to deal with the little stresses of life - before they stress you out. You must give yourself the best possible chance to come to the right decisions.

If you want to build a solid house then you make sure that you have really good foundations and a strong structure. The stronger the structure the less the house will be affected by internal or external stresses.

It's the same with us.

Our workouts will help you to build good foundations and a solid structure in your body and your mind.

Please use them!

Putting You in the Picture

**We're designed to deal with Big Stresses.
But – it's the Little Stresses that get us in the end.**

The Solution:

- *Don't panic!*

- *Find a reasoned response.*

- *Clear your mind.*

- *Then - make a genuine considered decision.*

Chapter 7
You Are What You Think

Using a Positive Attitude

*'Don't be what you've been –
be what you could be'.*

**We have all heard the statement 'you are what you eat'. There is much truth
in this: if you eat nothing but junk food high in saturated fat, sugars and salt
your body will look and feel terrible. No surprises there.**

The same is true of the statement 'you are what you do'. It makes sense that if
your job involves day-long heavy manual work you are going to have more muscle
from your job than someone who stays all day on the phone behind a desk. Your

average Canadian lumberjack is going to be a bit beefier than your pen pusher from Pennsylvania – unless our office worker does a bit more on the physical side.

So it should not be a surprise that what you think has an effect upon you. In other words:

'YOU ARE WHAT YOU THINK'

What do we mean by this? We believe that having a positive attitude about yourself and the world around you is the key to becoming a Picture of Health. But before we tell you exactly what we mean let us tell what we do not mean.

Firstly, we do not mean that if you just think that you are a pop star then you are a pop star and that you should win certain reality TV shows. We have all seen the contestants on those shows: a mixture of the truly talented, the terribly talentless and the downright mad. They all believe that they can be pop stars.

Or that if you think you are a brain surgeon so you can perform that tricky operation in your garage and save the hospital fees.

Or at 4ft 2 you can still be the greatest basketball player on earth.

This is not self-belief it is self-delusion and can be particularly unhealthy – especially to some unlucky brain surgery patient.

Secondly, we do not mean that just by thinking positively about something it is going to happen all by its self. That's not having a positive attitude, that is daydreaming. I'm not knocking dreams – we all have them and they have inspired mankind's greatest achievements. But the reason so many people like to daydream is because it is cheap, easy and safe! The total opposite of what is required to turn a dream into a reality.

Finally, we do not mean that you should become the eternal optimist: always looking on the bright side, never experiencing failure, wandering through this beautiful world a friend to everyone – and to small animals. That is not eternally optimistic – that is insanely optimistic!

Let's face it – life has its limits, its hard work and its downfalls. Anything else just isn't life.

So how can we say 'you are what you think?'

Well, when you think, you think about something. Be it the next trip away with the family, work, or whatever. It is the attitude you take to the things in your life, real or imagined, that have a huge effect on the way you see life and how people in your life see you. Here is one of our mottoes – commit this to memory –

CHANGE YOUR ATTITUDE TRANSFORM YOUR LIFE

We have all heard of tales of successful people whose attitude to life and the people around them became negative and their life spiralled down and they ended up broke and friendless.

By getting a more positive attitude to the people and things in your life you will feel great not only about yourself but about the things in your life too.

So let's start changing your attitude to the things in your life. But first a question: what is the most important thing in your life? We have asked this question many times and come up with some predictable and some scary answers:

'the children', 'my partner', 'family', 'the garden', 'my job', 'my classic car'.

Well we here at Picture of Health Clubs know the most important thing in your life; the answer may surprise and shock you, but the plain and simple answer is that the most important thing in your life is YOU.

I know what you are thinking, that's some ego you have; you're selfish – pretty small-minded of you. In a way you could be right especially if you bulldozed your way through life thinking of no one but yourself and what you can get out of it. But remember it is your life so you are bound to be in the centre, at the heart of it all. Here is a piece of wisdom:

LOVE YOUR NEIGHBOUR AS YOURSELF

By neighbour we do not mean the guy who lives next door but everybody we meet in life, family included.

Now, we cannot use this piece of logic to be nasty to our fellow man:

1. Love your neighbour as yourself.
2. I hate myself.
Conclusion: I hate my neighbour.

Nor can we put ourselves down so the people in our life will feel better – that's not love – that's just sad.

Before we can have a positive attitude to anything else in our lives we must start at the foundation of our lives – ourselves.

SELF IMAGE – YOU ARE WHAT YOU THINK

How do you see yourself? I don't mean rush to a mirror, but as we are there what do you see? How do you rate your looks on a scale of 1 to 10?

When you look at a half-filled glass is it half full or half empty?

Similarly:

When you look at your life is it half full or half empty?

Do you take a positive view of your life?

Do you take a positive attitude towards your life?

> *We believe that taking a positive attitude towards our lives is one of the key elements in our definition of Fitness.*

Well, we definitely do! We believe that taking a positive attitude towards our lives is one of the key elements in our definition of Fitness. Put simply, a negative attitude will eventually have a negative effect on your health and wellbeing – a positive attitude will enhance them.

To understand this allow us to explain how the brain works in our jargon-free Picture of Health Clubs way. This explanation will not get you through any psychology exams but you can understand the very basics.

We have to think positively because the brain is made to think positively. Let's have a few examples:

Think about a Christmas tree. what happens? 'PING': a picture of a Christmas tree pops into your head.

Now try this:
DO NOT think about a penguin with a red bow tie.
What happened? Did a picture of that penguin pop into your head?

Do not blame yourself if that penguin arrived dressed for the opera. That's how the brain works. It gravitates towards the images it creates. That's why when you say to someone 'do not drop that vase' the image of it dropping pops up into the brain and you can expect to hear a smash.

YOUR CONSCIOUS and SUB-CONSCIOUS MINDS

Let's look at them this way:

Imagine a captain on the bridge of his ship. He navigates the ship and sends his orders to the crew in the engine room. They control all the engines, instruments and machinery that run the ship - all the stuff the captain has no time to worry about. The men can't see where they are going; they just carry out the captain's orders. If the captain makes some error of judgement he could sink the ship.

Similarly, your conscious mind is the captain of your ship – your body. Your engine room – your sub-conscious mind receives the 'orders' from your conscious mind and carries them out.

The engine room crew on the ship automatically carries out the orders because he is the captain. He must be obeyed.

Now this relationship is not a one-way street. If the captain says 'go 1000 miles' and the engine room crew say 'there's only fuel for 500 miles' then no matter how much the captain yells 'go' the ship isn't going to go 1000 miles. The captain will have to change his plan.

It is the same with the sub-conscious mind. It advises us about our plans and our life. Usually, why we cannot do something.

The real difference between a ship and the mind is that if the captain wants the crew to do something, then he has to directly order it.

Your sub-conscious is not so discerning. Your sub-conscious mind will listen to all your conscious thoughts, speech and your doings and deal with them accordingly.

So if your thoughts are positive then your sub-conscious will store them and act positively.

Just like junk food harms the body – so junk thoughts harm the mind.

And if your thoughts are negative, your sub-conscious will store these negative thoughts and act accordingly.

For example - if you keep on saying to yourself 'I am not well' eventually your subconscious will accept these statements and eventually you will start to feel ill. Similarly, if you keep on saying to yourself 'I can't do this' then guess what, you won't do it because your sub-conscious will take on board your negative messages.

Just like junk food harms the body – so junk thoughts harm the mind.

You can therefore change your way of life by changing your thoughts and your attitude by feeding your sub-conscious mind only positive thoughts.

CHANGE YOUR ATTITUDE TRANSFORM YOUR LIFE

How many times have you heard a statement that says something like 'Our brains are immensely powerful yet we only use a very small percentage of their capacity'.

If you only used a little bit more than most of us normally use, then consider how much more you might achieve. Using the power of your sub-conscious mind is a very powerful way of tapping into this unused capacity.

> *The more that you use the same techniques the more familiar you will be with them and the more effective they will become.*

It is not complicated to send messages to your sub-conscious mind. You can do it any time, any place, anywhere. However, certain techniques and methods will provide a simple structure for you to work from. The more that you use the same techniques the more familiar you will be with them and the more effective they will become. Your sub-conscious will recognise these frequent messages and carry out your instructions more effectively. It's like learning to ride a bike. Eventually you will be cycling without thinking how you are doing it. Your sub-conscious has taken on board all the positive cycling rules and does it for you.

Your sub-conscious is there for you to command – don't waste it.

THE TECHNIQUES

I hope that you can now appreciate that taking a positive attitude towards your life is an integral part of being 'fit'.

In the Tool Box we will introduce you to simple workouts that will enable you to take a positive view on life.

Thinking Positive is a must if you want to become a Picture of Health.

A FINAL THOUGHT

Is your mind a muscle?

Well, obviously not – but – it's like a muscle.

The more you use it – the more it will grow.

And

If you don't use it - it will atrophy – it will waste away like a muscle does.

Remember, you are never too old to change your attitude, take on new ideas and change your habits.

Old dogs can learn new tricks.

FOOTNOTE: (I thought 'what a great way to explain the power of our sub-conscious mind by using the captain of the ship analogy'. Then I happened to browse through a book that I had not read for many years and there was the same analogy in black and white. Now there's an example of the power of the sub-conscious mind at work! The book is 'The Power of your Sub-conscious Mind' by Dr Joseph Murphy, first published in 1963).

Putting You in the Picture

- *Don't be what you've been - be what you could be.*
- *You are what you think.*
- *Change your attitude – transform your life.*
- *Your sub-conscious is there for you to command.*
- *Don't waste it!*

Chapter 8
Eating – Yes.
Dieting – No.

Even though I've been eating all my life I'm still no expert on diet and nutrition. I know we should all eat healthily but all the foods I love seem to be the bad ones. It did not matter years ago - I ate anything and everything and still stayed slim. I had less of a digestive system and more of an incinerator. But then I did more when I was younger – as a child I chased and caught balls, and as a teen I chased girls but never caught them! Now as an adult I'm chasing deadlines, but I'm not that slim anymore.

I started to read up on my diet - you are what you eat, right? I found that there is an awful lot of rubbish written about diet. Much of it is confusing or downright misleading. Most women's magazines include a new miracle diet every month, usually next to the recipe for chocolate cake. A suspicious person might think that the food and health industries are trying to keep us fat and on a diet.

Still, if we are to achieve Picture of Health Clubs status we definitely do have to consider diet and nutrition.

So here is some basic, down to earth, common sense, information for us Ordinary Folk to consider.

A major cause of concern for us ordinary people is undoubtedly all the problems that are caused through being overweight. It impacts on the way we look, feel, how we dress, and what we can do. It can affect our physical and mental health, job prospects, even our love life.

It comes as no surprise then that many of us go out and buy a diet book. Diet books are a sure way not only to loose weight but also a path to health, wealth and happiness.

But if you want all of the above, just go out and WRITE one.

Writing a new diet book is easy, it doesn't matter how far out it may seem – as long as you tell a good tale. Just try to include the following points -

1. Put an exotic location in the title. Malibu sounds good, how about 'The Hawaii Diet?'

2. Exclude or eat nothing but a certain food group. Cut out carbs or focus on fruit.

3. Explain that this can be done quickly, without exercise, and without too much sacrifice.

It will probably appeal to millions of us ordinary folk around the world who are looking for a quack, sorry, quick way to lose weight.

I guarantee that you will get loads of people saying how they swear by it - and lots more who swear at it, saying what a load of rubbish.
You should care? – as you continue to bank your royalty cheques.

Well some of us care – we have a conscience.

The truth is – most diets don't work in the long term. Invariably – they cannot be maintained for long periods – and then the dieter slips back into the old routine and rapidly regains weight. Off they go and buy the next gimmicky diet book, some of which are positively dangerous. This cycle of fast (the diet) and feast (falling back into your bad eating habits) is a sure way to alter your body for the worse.

YOU ARE WHAT YOU EAT

Our bodies are survival machines designed to survive the life of a caveman. So let us consider, for the moment, our bodies as another sort of machine: a car engine. If we want our car engine to have a long, problem-free life –then we must maintain it regularly and feed it a good quality fuel and oil.

In the case of us humans – the fuel we use are the calories we eat. (a calorie is actually a unit of heat – energy).

To work efficiently our body requires sufficient intake of calories (energy) each day to balance the energy used up - spent on our activities. The energy used up depends on our age, size, occupation, exercise, etc. The average is 1500 – 2500.

Before you rush out and buy your daily calorie intake in chocolate bars do not forget that, like a car you need both fuel and oil. 'Oil' for us comes in the form of protein, vitamins, minerals, fibre and all the other stuff that comes from good balanced diet. In short we also need nutrients. Just like cars, our bodies will not function without fuel but will go quite a way without oil (nutrients) until the engine seizes - permanently.

Now that we know roughly how many calories you need every day then weight loss should be a simple piece of arithmetic. An average size man who doesn't do any exercise and sits at a desk all day uses up about 2500 calories a day. Therefore – if he eats 2500 calories in his food – he will be in a state of energy balance – and his weight should remain constant.

If he goes on a diet and takes in say – only 2000 calories a day he should lose weight.

Yes – but.

I told you that your body is a survival machine – one designed for surviving in the world of the caveman. When the dieting body is faced with a shortage of food it goes into 'starvation' mode - as it looks for the missing 500 calories to balance the books. Firstly it will find it in fluids and your lean muscle tissue, especially ones hardly used. It will save the fat for later (the famine syndrome).

When the diet stops and you start to put on weight – which you will:

- *You will replace the fluids.*

- *And your extra weight will come back as fat.*

- *You won't replace that lean muscle tissue - after all why replace something you never use?*

If you want that lean muscle tissue to come back then you will have to exercise – ugh!

The other problem with dieting is that your metabolic rate will slow down. The metabolic rate is the rate at which your body burns calories – a bit like the idling speed on a car's engine.

As your metabolic rate slows down you will have less and less energy and your body will continue to store higher levels of body fat with all its ensuing problems you build up for the future. Remember our bodies are survival machines designed to keep us alive through lean times.

Thus the only way to short-circuit the famine syndrome and make our body lose weight and shift unwanted fat is to do the following:

BURN UP CALORIES AS FUEL by EXERCISING

Don't panic – yet! There will be no need to join a gym, jog or wear lycra - though what you do in the privacy of your own home is your own business. Read the chapter on FITNESS TRAINING later.

EATING WELL - (I don't mean dining in five star restaurants!)

One of the secrets to being healthy is to eat high quality fuel. Drop the pie - I said quality not quantity! High quality food will give you more energy, motivate you more and help to reduce your stress levels.

Q. What is high quality food?

A. Food that will supply you with all the calories and nutrients that you need, in the right quantities and the right balance.

Q. What is low quality food?

A. Those foods with limited nutritional value but loaded with calories, sometimes called junk foods.

A better definition of junk food may be 'Any foods that are high in salt, sugar, fat or calories and low nutrient content'.

Good examples of these so-called 'empty calorie' foods are salted snack foods, sweets, most sweet desserts, fried fast food and carbonated drinks. Generally they offer little in terms of proteins, vitamins and minerals – but lots in calories from sugars and fats.

A good rule of thumb guide is to look at the nutritional facts label to see if sugar, fat or salt are one of the first three ingredients. Ingredients are listed in descending order of magnitude - biggest first. So if they are listed that high in the list of ingredients then you can probably consider that food to be too high in sugar, fat or salt.

DON'T GET ME WRONG – I'm not saying don't eat low quality food. Let's be honest we all do it – and we all obviously enjoy it. But we should be aware of what we are eating, what it may be doing to our waistband and other parts of our body (internal and external) – At the very least – we should CUT BACK.

A GOOD BALANCED DIET should have the right mixture of carbohydrates, proteins and fats.
You should eat good energy giving foods. You should avoid high-fat and sugar laden foods that can be addictive.
You should try to eat as much fresh food and fruit as you can.

PROCESSED FOODS AND PREPARED MEALS

I know that these are the easy option – after all who wants to cook after a hard day at work? If you do buy these then you should look at the nutritional facts labels – once you get past the basic food ingredients you will see lists of all sorts of chemical additives with weird-sounding names and E numbers. A good rule of thumb is that the longer the list is and the more unpronounceable the additive is – the more you should consider not buying the product!

RECOMMENDATION – Follow the eating tips in the food tool. Plus there are many good recipe books on the market that will help to ensure you have a good healthy low fat, good nutrient diet.

But BEWARE of the strange low-calorie diets and all the other peculiar oddities that you will see in the bookshop.

AIM – Our aim is for a balanced diet but modern Western diets tend to be out of balance because they contain too much of the wrong type of foods. With guidance from the food tool you can produce a healthy, balanced and tasty diet.

DIETING – Having given you some sound advice about food and how to lose weight, i.e. fewer calories and a bit more activity, you would be forgiven for thinking that we advocate a strict calorie counting regime. Well you'd be wrong.

The calorie counting path is taken by the majority of 'fat clubs' that meet weekly across the country. Each club brand has its own way to count calories to make it easier for you. However, most require you to weigh food and note what you have eaten. Eventually, with your scales permanently out and charts and notes hung up, your kitchen looks more like a clinic.

Don't think for one moment that I'm knocking these clubs. The vast majority of them are well run and backed by international franchises. The leader of the club is often a successful slimmer who encourages the group with her experiences of success and failures at slimming. In fact this is the major strength of 'fat clubs': mutual support from club leader and members, plus all the franchise support with recipe books and slimmer's treats that they sell. (Still check that label) It is no wonder that these clubs are both popular and successful. But there is a big downside to these clubs, which can be unhealthy.

The problem with 'fat clubs' is the conflict between human nature and the weekly weighing session. At the weekly weighing sessions the slimmers line up before the club leader like sinners before St. Peter awaiting judgment. The judgment of weight lost, gained or stayed the same has as profound effect on our slimmer as any judgment made by the apostle.

Should the verdict be weight lost, then it is a time for celebration - and why not. You have struggled with this damn diet for a whole week (it felt like a fortnight). You lost weight. Time for some real food!

Those who have lost weight treat themselves to forbidden food and a bit of booze to celebrate. The day after, they tot up the calories scoffed on their feast and realize that to stay on the plan, they have to live off carrots until next weigh day.

Here our hapless slimmer is on the fast and feast type of diet we warned you about at the beginning of this chapter: only the cycle is every week. At least the news for the binge slimmer was good: weight loss. For those who have religiously followed the diet and have stayed the same or – heaven forbid – put pounds on, the news can be quite depressing and they give up. And that's a shame because they could have made real progress if they had just stuck with it.

We advocate a new way of eating rather than a diet. This can be found in the Food Tool. This will give you advice on the size and portions you need.

HAPPY EATING.

PART II

Chapter 9
Getting Out of Bed in the Morning – UGGHH!

The Best Way to Start the Day

*'If we were supposed to pop out of bed in the morning
we would all sleep in toasters!'*

**Everybody is different. Some of us are night people. And some of us are
morning people.**

Morning people can spring out of bed in the early hours full of the joys of spring
– raring to go.

The rest of us – open our eyes ever so slowly, groan, then wish we could turn over and go back to sleep for a few more hours. We drag ourselves out of bed in a daze, feeling weak and stiff as board – and dreading the start to another day's activity.

But it doesn't have to be like that – even for people like us.

Because it's all in our mind.

And we can retrain our minds.

However – we may need to change a few habits.

Before we go any further, please answer a few questions:

1. **How do you describe your mornings?**
    A. One mad rush between bed and work.
    B. Don't know - never fully awake.
    C. A time to refuel the body and prepare for the day ahead.

2. **What is the snooze button for?**
    A. A chance to grab an extra 10 minutes sleep.
    B. A chance to grab an extra 20 minutes sleep.
    C. Not sure – I'm always up before the alarm goes off.

3. **How do you describe your breakfast?**
    A. Coffee on the run.
    B. Eh.... breakfast?
    C. The most important meal of the day.

4. **How do you describe your commute to work?**
    A. With words that would make a sailor blush.
    B. The storm before the calm.
    C. A necessary evil.

If your answers were mainly As or Bs then join the club with 80% of the population. (Some people on my morning train are so miserable I think it could be 100%) If you answered mainly Cs, well done. I'm sure Oscar Wilde was not thinking of you when he said 'only dull people are brilliant at breakfast.'

Most of us suffer the stress and tension of commuting to work.
It's no wonder that once we get to work, we are already stressed out and full of tension – and the day has barely started.

Let's suggest an alternative routine – which with very little effort we can easily master.

I guarantee:

- *It will change your life.*

- *Give you much more energy all day.*

- *Reduce your stress levels.*

And

- *Enable you to be much more focused for your day's activities.*

THE FIRST STEP

The first thing you need to do is give yourself a little extra time in the morning. You will probably say, 'I haven't got it!'

Dare I say – go to bed a little earlier and change the time on your alarm call! - and then actually get out of bed when the alarm goes off rather than having a multitude of snooze!

Once you get into your new routine, you won't need the alarm call. Your own internal alarm call will tell you when it is time – because you will want to get up.

So the first step to your new wake up routine actually starts the night before by getting a good night's sleep.

However if you have spent the previous night in a wild debauchery of sex, drugs and drink even my workouts probably won't work.

It's probably best to save those activities for the weekend.

The WAKEUP workouts are very simple and are summarised as follows:

1. **Wake up!**

2. **Take a few moments to think about the day ahead.**

3. **Work through a short stretching routine (The Bedstretcher Workout) as you lie in bed.**

4. **Get showered/washed/dressed.**

5. **Breakfast. Yes, your mother was right! Breakfast is the most important meal of the day.**

6. **Leave the house – but with a difference.**

OK, That was the summary now here is the detail:

1. Wake Up

So you've just woken up – now what do you do? Well first of all let's hope that you've had a decent night's sleep. It goes without saying that if you have been practising some of my suggestions in my chapter 'Why Can't I Get a Decent Night's Sleep?', then you are more likely to have had a good sleep.

If the alarm has woken you then press the snooze button. This will give you ten minutes to complete the next few tasks without running the risk of nodding off and oversleeping.

As you start to come round the first thing to do is to clear your head and start to focus on the new day.

2. Focus on the new day

Sit up in bed and take a few gentle slow deep breaths in and out. Begin to feel your body and your mind shaking off your drowsiness. Start to focus on the day ahead and take a few moments for a quiet review.

If you made some affirmations or some positive thoughts the night before then you should quietly repeat them to yourself just to ensure that your sub-conscious has filed them in the right place. Just a brief reminder to reinforce those messages is all that is required.

If you did not do some stuff the night before then I suggest you just give yourself three positive suggestions to set yourself up for the day.

If your thoughts are too negative then you may not want to get out of bed at all! If you have to face a nasty task that day then focus on the benefits of getting it done. If that does not work then focus on a treat you can give to yourself when you complete it – we are all open to a bit of bribery.

Here are some positive suggestions:

- *I am going to have a good day.*
- *My concentration will be 100% throughout the day.*
- *I always feel fine and in control all day – no matter what.*

You will think of many more to suit your needs. Just make sure that whatever you say is totally positive.

'I would like to have a nice day' will not do.

Alternatively you might consider choosing one of the following Workouts from the Tool Box: Mind Focus or Mind Power Tools.

So that's the mental stuff sorted, next we must consider your physical body. This lump of flesh and bone has been lying in bed for the last 7 or 8 hours (10 to 12 hours if you are a teenager) and apart from some tossing and turning has been fairly still. So, you are bound to be feeling stiff to one degree or another. One thing is for sure – the older you get – the stiffer you will feel. Sorry, but that's a fact of life, so we must do as much as we can to ease away that stiffness in an easy sensible way.

3. Don't dive out of bed

This is the worst thing that you can do, especially on cold mornings. So many people do this and then they wonder why on earth they have pulled some muscles or strained various parts of their anatomy.

Our bodies are like car engines – they perform better and last longer when they have been looked after. Would you dream of jumping into your car switch on the engine and then drive off at top speed? Maybe you would! – but if you want to look after your car you should allow the engine to warm up first before putting your foot down on the accelerator.

Of course, should you find yourself in someone else's bed and hear a key in the door then jumping out of bed and into a wardrobe or out of a window could be the best option.

Gentle Stretching in Bed

Once we have come around and know what day it is then it's time for a gentle stretch. Have you ever seen a cat stretch after a period of inactivity or sleep? See how effortlessly it stretches out its body; first each leg in turn and then the other parts of its body. Basically you should do the same. It will only take you a few minutes, it is very simple to do and will give you an immediate benefit.

I call this little routine 'The **BEDSTRETCHER WORKOUT**'

You will find a full description of the Bedstretcher Workout in The Tool Box.

I have taught this workout to so many people and the feedback is always the same. They are amazed how doing such a simple workout as this transforms their start to the day.

The workout is not too vigorous – you do not want to disturb the person next to you – and it's not too long – your bladder will tell you how long is too long.

OK – you've done the Bedstretcher Workout; you're feeling great and now you have to perform the next major task of the day – getting out of bed!

Why is it a major task? You just get out of bed!

Sure, and when you are young and fit it's not a problem. But as we get older or we are suffering from some physical disability, we find that we have to do it with much more care because all of a sudden it's no longer that easy any more.

Here is a safe way to get out of bed:

- *Lie adjacent to the side of the bed.*
- *Turn on to your side facing the edge of the bed.*
- *Pull both knees up towards your chest.*
- *Swivel your feet over the edge of the bed to the floor.*
- *At the same time raise yourself to the sitting position by gently pushing your upper body up with your hands.*
- *You are now sitting on the edge of the bed in an upright position.*
- *Arch your body forward slightly, place your feet on the floor and then raise yourself up by using your arms pushing down on the mattress.*
- *You are now standing up out of bed without any strain or effort at all.*
- *Easy? And safe.*

4. Get Showered/Washed/Dressed

I hope we do not need to give you hints on these!

5. Eat breakfast

Breakfast is by and far the most important meal of the day. When your body was asleep you were not eating. It stands to reason you should break your fast as soon as you can with good quality food. This will crank up your metabolic rate and you will start to burn more calories during the day.

6. Leaving the House

We are now ready to start our day and join the big world just waiting for us outside the protection of the front door of our house.

When I say, 'Leaving the House' I really mean switching from domestic mode into work mode.

Of course if you are a home worker then you will not be physically leaving the house. But you will alter your mental out look to focus on the tasks ahead – be it the children challenge - getting them washed, fed and to school on time, or facing the tidal wave of e-mails about to appear on the computer when you finally build up enough courage to turn it on.

Inner Smile Workout

A very good workout to do as you 'leave the house' is to practise the Inner Smile Tool. This will set you up nicely for the day.

You are ready to leave the house, you have your coat on, you have your briefcase, handbag, lunchbox, toolbox, etc. with you and you're ready to go.

Look at yourself in the hall mirror (Why does everyone have a hall mirror?). Yes – I know – horrible isn't it! Especially if you haven't washed, shaved, or put your 'face' on.

Then just practise this simple routine. It will soon become second nature to you and it will remain with you all of the day.

(See The Tool Box – The Inner Smile Workout)

LEAVE THE HOUSE AND HAVE A GREAT DAY!

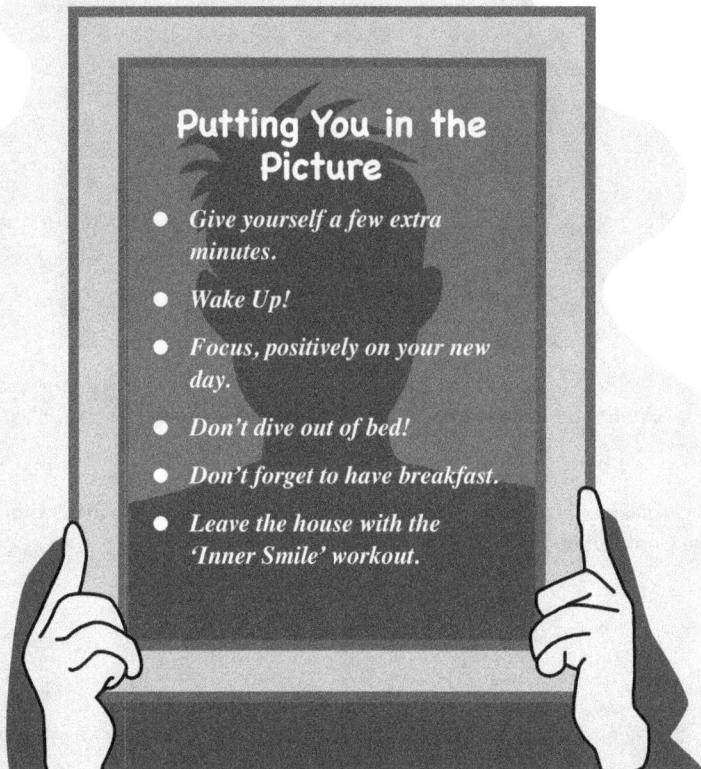

Putting You in the Picture

- *Give yourself a few extra minutes.*
- *Wake Up!*
- *Focus, positively on your new day.*
- *Don't dive out of bed!*
- *Don't forget to have breakfast.*
- *Leave the house with the 'Inner Smile' workout.*

Chapter 10
Commuting

How to Arrive At Work – Really Stressed!

'Commuter – one who spends his life in riding to and from his wife'.
E. B. White

Our occasional series looking at the wildlife around us: we focus this time on The Commuter.

Commuters (Travellus Stressus)

Distribution

Found around the Western World usually within an hour of a big city. Plumage varies but the species can be easily recognised by its call of tuts and sighs. The species favours nesting in sub-urban areas.

Migratory Habits

Tends to leave the nest in the morning to travel to the city where it occupies itself in acquiring things for its brood. Returns to the nest at evening, sometimes way after sundown.

Subspecies

Subspecies are defined by their mode of migration. Two of the most common are described below: -

Trainus Stressus

These can be easily identified by their habit of flocking very close together – mostly whilst standing. A characteristic of the sub-species is the hi-fi mating dance with its characteristic head-bobbing. Another telltale sign is its evening call of 'I'm on the train'.

Auto Stressus

These can be seen in great slow moving migratory columns that appear in the morning and the evening. The species is very protective of its territory and warn other members that they are too close with its raucous 'beeeep' warning call. This may be accompanied by the exhibiting of the 'finger' warning display.

Commuting is a modern problem. The idea of travelling an hour or more to work would have horrified our grandparents. They preferred to live a comfortable distance from the farm, factory or shop. But times change.

People do not want to live in a factory zone. They prefer to live away from their place of work for a number of reasons: better housing, better schools for their children or simply the fact that they cannot afford a house in the big city. For the foreseeable future commuting is here to stay.

With the best will in the world, we cannot shorten the distance you commute or speed up the journey but we can make the trip a little less stressful.

First things first: I want to define the commuting trip. 'That's fairly easy', I hear you say. 'It's how long it takes you to travel from the house to work or work to home.' Well, in a way that's true but I want to add a little more. I define the commuting trip as the time it takes you to make the trip plus the time it takes you to recover from that trip.

Recovery time makes sense if you ran or bicycled to work. Your body needs time to recover from the physical activity of the commute and depending on the commute and your fitness it could take a few minutes, half an hour or even days.

Most of us commute by transport for a number of reasons: length of trip, the weather, safety, or because we are just a little lazy. But just because there is no physical exertion it doesn't mean that there is no recovery time. Most of us encounter stress when we commute. Not allowing yourself full recovery time after your commute can affect your next activity. You are irritable in work or grouchy when you get home. Adding recovery time to your commute allows you to accurately assess the impact of the journey on your life. It also means you enter the next task without all the stress from the trip hindering you.

> *Not allowing yourself full recovery time after your commute can affect your next activity.*

We are going to focus on two types of commuting, the car, where you are in charge, and the train, where you travel. We cannot make your journey any shorter and we cannot make it quicker but our hints and techniques can reduce stress and make that daily trek, if not enjoyable, at least tolerable.

THE CAR

You have seen the commercials: the car streaks along the open road. No other car in sight, just the driver against nature. Man and machine in perfect harmony.

Well today's driving is more chaos than harmony. I do not know where these car advertisers live but it's nowhere near me. Year by year the situation is getting worse. There have been initiatives by pressure groups and government: car sharing, congestion charges, and new roads that quickly fill up. With no viable alternative in the form of public transport it looks like we will be with the car for quite a long time.

If we cannot change the congestion on the roads then what else can we change? If it is possible you could change the time that you need to commute so that you miss the rush hour both in and out of work. However not many of us have a sympathetic boss who will let us do this. After all he may not want you to start work at 7am if the shop you work in does not open until 9.

With every other factor unable to be changed there is only one alternative left to you and that is the most important one – you.

Most people's reaction to commuting is very human. They hate it and it is an intrusion on the time you can spend with your family. So they leave it until the last minute to set off to work so that they can spend a few extra minutes at home (getting a home is the main reason why we work, so why not enjoy it?). After work we race home to the loving embrace of our family. During this race to and from home it seems that the whole of humanity is trying to get in your way. You know the types:

The shirt-sleeved salesman type in the company car. They are always in a hurry chasing targets and clients and cutting up anybody to get their bonus. Just feel sorry for these poor pathetic creatures and let them go on their way. After all if they meet their target this year they may get a company car that has indicators as standard and not as an optional extra.

Kamikaze pizza deliverymen weaving through traffic on small mopeds, delivering their pizza with the urgency of an ambulance delivering a long-awaited donor organ. Give this poor minimum wage soul a wide berth – after all he may be a student working his way through medical school and this, and free pizzas, may be his only way of sustaining himself.

White van man tearing at break-neck speeds to his next job. Just remember how many times you have waited in vain for a tradesman to call so let him rush to his next job.

All these people are in a rush and they are stressing themselves and other road users out of their head by rushing. What we propose is a different form of driving which we call centred driving.

Centred Driving

Centred driving is a technique that allows us to get from A to B safely and with the minimum amount of stress. As human beings we all a bit self-centred. You may have heard of the proverb 'An Englishman's home is his castle'. Well many people transfer this attitude to car driving. However cars do not have 6ft thick walls of granite: they and their contents are much more fragile. To change you from a 'self-centred driver' to a 'centred driver' we need to consider three aspects of driving.

Time – it stands to reason that if you have not allowed yourself enough time to make your journey then you have to drive like a maniac to arrive on time. How much time you need will depend on the length, time of day and roads available for your journey. Experiment with this by giving yourself an extra ten to twenty minutes to begin with. Allowing this extra time means that you can encounter delays and still arrive without the stress of being late.

Speed – giving yourself extra time means that you can slow down. Apart from saving fuel and wear and tear on the car (it's all money) the journey becomes less of a rush and therefore relaxing. Try cruising in the slow lane at 55-60 rather than hogging the middle lane at 70. You will be surprised that it does not add that much to your journey and you will feel much more relaxed in your driving.

Attitude – This is the main difference between the centred and the self-centred driver. Consideration for other road users and not being bloody minded about the rules of the road can reduce stress and make your journey more pleasant. Let's have a few examples:

Scenario 1
A driver cuts you up for no apparent reason.

Self-Centred Driver – hit the horn! Then tailgate that sonofabitch with your headlights on full beam. That'll teach the jerk. Then if you suspect him of being a jerk he could very well decide to slam on those brakes and your insurance premiums will go through the roof as you go through his rear bumper.

Centred Driver – forget the horn and abuse and concentrate on your driving. Keep a safe distance from him just in case he does something else stupid. If you still feel annoyed by the idiot when you get home then secretly hope he bumps into someone as stupid as him when he's driving home. Then forget about him. This may be a bit mean but, as drivers we are centred not saints.

Scenario 2
Some idiot is driving whilst talking on her mobile phone without using a hands-free set. She's all over the place causing you to hit the brakes.

Self Centred Driver – lean on your horn so it sounds like an ocean liner leaving port and struggle to catch the jerk's eye so that you can give her a withering look to punish her. Doing this you will be taking your own eyes off the road but it's different for you, right?

Centred Driver – honk your horn so that the driver knows that she's driving dangerously. Don't hang on the horn; just enough to let her know that no phone call is important enough to cause a crash. Hopefully she or the person on the other end will hang up. Keep your distance just in case that phone call is that important!

Scenario 3
You're on the motorway. Lane closures have been announced for the last 2 miles. All the other motorists have joined the open lane ages ago and it is getting full. Your lane is backed up; the other, soon to be closed, lane is not but the road works are getting closer: 400 yds, 200 yds. Suddenly some flash git tears along the next lane stops just ahead of you, having sped past all the other sad fools waiting in the line behind, and signals for you to let him in.

Self-centred drive – don't let the motorist merge: why does he think that he has priority over everyone else? Keep very close to the car in front so that there is no room for him to cut in. This way it will teach him to be more considerate and he will have to get some other fool behind you to let him in.

Centred driver – just let him in. Afterall it's not your job in life to teach him a lesson – that just makes you look just as bad as him. And keeping him out may force him to do something stupid like aiming for a gap that is too small and it could cause a bump.

If keeping yourself safe and stress free isn't enough of an incentive to keep you from trying to penalise delinquent motorists, just think of all those higher premiums that make the insurance companies a healthy profit.

TRAIN TRAVEL

Train travel, or any form of travel where we ride as a passenger can cause stress when we are delayed. This usually presents itself as anger because we are not in control of the situation. Though if I was in an aircraft at 30,000 ft and the stewardess asked me to take control of the plane I would rather leave it to the professionals.

Being delayed is annoying. At least with the advent of mobile phones we can ring home and avoid a burnt dinner. There is not much we can do to remedy the situation: we can shout, rave, seethe and sigh as much as we like but no amount of doing this will move a 400 tonne train if it has broken down.

Remaining stoical is the only answer and if you still feel miffed when you get home you can write a letter of complaint to the company involved. Just look at it as a variation of the writing tool we describe in the tool box.

> *Look at the time spent on a train as time to do something constructive.*

Being stuck on a train can be mind-numbingly dull. The same people taking the same journey at the same time past the same houses. Look at the time spent on the train as time to do something constructive. Here are a few examples used by friends and family during the commute:

Learn a language – listen to the tapes whilst you move and read the textbook. Just do not speak out loud on the crowded train as people think that you are mad.

Read – catch up with the latest novel or news via a newspaper.

Talk – meeting the same people every day can lead to a friendship. One friend has what she calls her 'train club' and her gang even goes out for social evenings every so often.

Catch up with work – use this time to prepare for a presentation or read up on your notes.

Chill out – that way when I get home I am ready for the family problems.

An ideal time to practise some of the Tools.

Whatever you do, use this time constructively and then it will not be wasted.

So we have tried to show you in a light-hearted way that you have choices with your commuting.

Arrive at work or your destination really stressed out, and then waste even more time trying to pull yourself together.

Or

Arrive at work or your destination full of energy, totally relaxed and raring to go.

THE CHOICE IS YOURS!

Putting You in the Picture

- *Commuting = travel time + recovery time.*
- *Become a centred driver.*
- *Train commuting – do something constructive.*

Chapter 11
During Your Day

Is It Time to Hit the Pause Button?

'Every now and then go away; ever briefly have a little relaxation, for when you come back to work your judgment will be surer, since to remain constantly at work will cause you to lose power'.

Leonardo Da Vinci

What do you do for a living?

Are you a manual worker? Are you an office worker? Do you spend many hours behind the wheel of a motor vehicle? Are you a busy housewife?

What ever you do you use your muscles - and you are using them in particular ways that are appropriate to your job. So hour after hour after hour your muscles are working hard on your behalf to support your particular job function.

It doesn't matter what job you are doing; some of your muscles are working harder than others to support that job function. Your body, an economical survival machine that is designed to adapt to whatever job you do, will strengthen the muscles that you use during your workday. The body also ignores the muscles that you do not use. After all, why go to all that effort to maintain something you do not use?

So over a period of time your whole body and all your muscles will adjust to the fact that some of your muscles work harder and more often than others.

'That sounds fine' - I hear you say - but I say 'No'.

Here's why.

Say you sit at a desk for seven/eight hours a day. Your muscles adjust to your particular working posture. In fact over time some of these muscles will actually shorten in length (foreshorten) because they become accustomed to your normal working/sitting posture. You eventually stand up and what happens. These shortened muscles are then forced to stretch themselves beyond their comfort zone.

Then what? Stiffness, cramps, aches and pains in various parts of your body. (Remember the OOH – AAH Test?).

There is a significant danger of your body losing more and more of its flexibility and mobility the longer you allow it to remain in a particular posture without taking some remedial action. Without taking some remedial action there can be a danger of you developing a long-term chronic problem.

A similar scenario exists for any job that you do – for manual workers, even for sportspeople.

You must have seen sportsmen and women stretching out their bodies before and after their sports. Ever wondered why? No matter how fit or super fit these sportsmen and women are, their chosen sport will demand an excess use of particular muscles in a particular way: the leg muscles of an Olympic power lifter need explosive power whilst a marathon runner needs endurance and stamina.

For those of use at the other end of the sporting scale watching somebody play golf is probably a good example of using particular muscles only – all that twisting and turning is quite obvious.

> *So just as 'you are what you eat' your body, will develop to cope only with the job – in other words 'you are what you do!'*

All this is great news for the muscles that develop but bad news for the muscles that are ignored. This means that the neglected muscles are storing up problems for us in the future when we want to do things other than our job – which is why we work, right?

Now I hope that I am not panicking you. If I am, I apologise, for that is not my intention.

I am just trying to advise you in a simple way that whatever you do you should be looking after all of your body.

And of course 'All of your body' includes your brain, your mind.

Consider that during the day your muscles are working for you and they are building up stress and tension; isn't the same thing happening to your mind?

Well – 'Yes'.

We can all only concentrate for a limited period of time. Then our mind starts to wander and our productivity and our effectiveness reduces. The longer we continue to concentrate then the more stress/tension will build up in our system.

Eventually we concentrate so hard on trying to concentrate that we end up being unable to concentrate on what we should be concentrating on. Did your mind wander then? I think that mine did! It's time for a solution.

So what do we do? Well - it's all very simple!

Here is the answer: WE HIT THE PAUSE BUTTON.

Whatever you do during the day you should hit the pause button and give yourself a break every couple of hours or so. The break will only consist of a few minutes, maybe only a minute or two. That's all it will take. So, even all you workaholics and terribly busy people will be able to do it. In fact it will improve your performance! So ignore it at your peril.

Just a couple of minutes every hour or so and it will help to transform your life! During these couple of minutes you will

● *Unwind your body and your mind.*

● *Get rid of all that tension and stress that is constantly trying to build up in your body and your mind.*

Here is what you do:

● *The 'AM/PM/Anytime Workout' – definitely. This simple and gentle workout will ease out all the tension that has built up in your body.*

● *'Mind Focus' tool workout – definitely. The simple way to 'unstress' your mind and give yourself an injection of relaxation. If you are feeling a bit uptight or feeling a bit stressed then do the 'Mind Clearing' workout instead.*

That's all there is to it. Do these simple workouts as regularly as you can.

Soon – they will become second nature to you.

Soon – you will be doing them without even thinking about it.

Immediately – you will feel transformed.

Putting You in the Picture

- *Avoid losing flexibility and mobility.*

- *'You are what you do'.*

- *We can only concentrate for a limited period of time.*

- *Hit the Pause Button.*

- *Unwind your body and mind.*

- *Get rid of all your stress and tension.*

- *Do the Workouts regularly.*

Chapter 12
PM Blues

The Usual Afternoon Energy Slump!

Come the afternoon and most people's internal spring starts to wind down: we feel tired, we watch the clock; work feels a little more difficult, the time goes more slowly.

Some people believe that we are programmed to feel a little dozy in the afternoons and need a little nap – just like cats do. However unless you are working for a Mexican, the chances of having a siesta in the modern world are practically nil.

If you can grab a nap in your job (make sure it's for twenty minutes maximum), then that's great. It's not a good idea for a bus driver but then neither is it a good career move to doze in an office with an eagle-eyed boss!

If, like the rest of us, you have a job where you cannot nap then we have to beat the blues another way.

Reasons why we hit the PM Blues

1. We run out of steam.

Perhaps we skipped breakfast, had too little lunch or had the wrong sort of food. Basically we are running out of calories and therefore energy. This does not mean that we are going to die of starvation but if there is less blood sugar in the body, then the body will use its reserves of fuel – fat.

Now when it comes to fat some of us seem to have more reserves than Fort Knox so you would be forgiven for thinking that using fat in this way is a good thing. When the body shifts its gear from blood sugar to fat we get a slump – just when we shift a car from a higher to a lower gear – the car, and our body slow down. We get less done, feel like doing less and eventually burn less calories.

Beat the blues by having breakfast and lunch – do not go for a sugar hit: chocolate bars and the like. Rather aim for foods that are 'slow burning' to give you energy during the day. Such 'slow burn' foods are complex carbohydrates – and like all things complex it takes time to break it down. Such foods as brown rice, wholemeal breads and pasta are the best. But there is a huge choice out there.
(See 'Eating – Yes: Dieting – No' and the Food Tool for further information)

2. We have too big a lunch – maybe with some alcohol.

Tell me, what would you rather do: work hard or have a large meal, dessert, and some wine? If, like me, you opted for the meal over the work are you surprised that your body would rather use its energy to digest that feast than concentrate on paperwork?

Eating a large lunch is a sure way to the PM Blues. Alcohol is a depressant so it will slow you down. Beat the blues – keep to a light lunch with no alcohol. If you have to have a heavy business lunch then make sure you conclude the business before the cheese and biscuits – and keep the rest of the day free to slump!

3. Caffeine - the yo-yo drink.

Caffeine from coffee, tea and cola will certainly bring you out of the PM Blues. It is an instant pick me up. But what goes up must come down and when the caffeine runs out the PM Blues will be bluer! The same effect happens with high sugar bars – you get the hit followed by the slump.

Beat the blues – now I will not be a hypocrite and tell you to avoid caffeine and confectionery – a good cup of black coffee and some dark chocolate is one of my treats in life. It is a good, if temporary, way to beat the PM Blues and I use it as a treat after finishing a nasty job. Just remember that the only way to beat tiredness is to sleep and drinking coffee late in the day can disrupt your sleep at night.

4. Lack of oxygen, stuffy atmosphere, lack of fresh air.

A stuffy workplace can drag you down. Work can wear you down – after all if work was so good wouldn't the rich keep it for themselves? After 6 hours in the office is it no wonder that people get the PM Blues?

Beat the blues – escape! I do not mean jumping out of the window, running along the fire escape and joining the circus – well, not quite yet.

> *Always take a lunch break. Working through your lunch break will not get any more work done.*

Escape physically from the work place: always take a lunch break. Working through your lunch break will not get any more work done – you will slump in the afternoon. Get away from the desk, go outside if you can and get some fresh air into your lungs.

Escape mentally. I do not mean you dreaming of yourself on a secluded beach with that young film star. Rather do one of our workouts. You will return to your work refreshed and relaxed.

Other ways to beat the PM Blues

Change your environment.

Open a window, add a plant. Do an office environment audit to identify and change the surroundings you work in for the better. I admit it is easier to change the surroundings in your executive office than a steel works.

Change your work schedule.

If you suffer with the PM Blues and all our tips do not help then change your work schedule to take this into account. If you run out of inspiration in the afternoon then leave the mundane jobs until then. If you are looking for the buzz in the PM then leave the stimulating jobs until then to spur you on. You know your job; you know your Blues. Adapt.

Most important:

DO THE AM/PM/ANYTIME WORKOUT REGULARLY

Putting You in the Picture

- *The usual afternoon energy slump.*
- *Run out of steam.*
- *Too big a lunch – with alcohol?*
- *Caffeine – the yo-yo drink.*
- *Lack of Oxygen.*
- ✔ *Change your environment.*
- ✔ *Change your work schedule.*
- ✔ *Do the AM/PM/Anytime workout regularly.*

Chapter 13
Evening Exhaustion

The 'Time Out Principle'

Remember Chapter Two? 'My Old Typical Day'

It's been another hard day's grind, commuting to work – train always late: waste of time rushing. Commuting back home – takes forever. The ongoing stresses of that job; you're definitely overworked and underpaid, etc. etc. At last you've arrived home to that haven of family bliss. You are looking forward to a bit of peace – no chance! That's impossible because you're immediately involved in family things.

Remember Chapter Three? 'My New Typical Day'

It's been another hard day's grind, commuting to work – train always late: waste of time rushing. Commuting back home – takes forever. The ongoing stresses of that job; you're definitely overworked and unpaid, etc. etc.
At last you've arrived home to that haven of family bliss. You are looking forward to a bit of peace – no chance! That's impossible because you're immediately involved in family things!

They're the same aren't they? Yes, but there is a difference.
If you have forgotten, then look back at Chapters Two and Three again and refresh your memory.

OK, you've spotted it? In Chapter Three our character took a 'time out'. Five minutes to be precise to switch from stressed worker to head of the household.

Let's go back to basics. Complete this simple questionnaire to check your stress levels when arriving home:

1. When you get home are you:
    a. like a creature from another planet?
    b. too tired to know what planet you are on?
    c. so happy to be home that you feel on cloud nine?

2. When you get home do you feel:
    a. like you have just ran a marathon whilst trying to learn Swahili?
    b. like you have lost to a chess and a kung fu master?
    c. physically relaxed and mentally alert?

3. Does commuting feel like:
    a. you are driving in a stock car race, blind folded?
    b. you are building the railway rather than travelling on it?
    c. a chance to finish that novel?

If you answered C to the questions then you don't need to read the rest of this chapter. Well done!

If, like me, you answered A or B to the questions then please read on.

The truth is that most of us are working harder, with longer hours, with more stress, and more commuting than ever before. And if we commute by car then our driving is probably driving us bonkers from all the time we spend just stuck in traffic! (See chapter on Commuting).

So by the time we get home we are entitled to be just a little frayed at the edges.

Now for the purposes of this little chat let's assume that our partner, wife, husband has been working at home all day and/or looking after kids, dog, cat, etc.

You arrive home, the family is delighted to see you walk through the door because they love you and missed you! Aah! So naturally they immediately want to tell you about all the really 'exciting' things that are going on in their lives today and generally catch up with everything since you were all last together.

Why can't they understand that you are tired/exhausted/had a lousy day at the office/had an awful journey to/from work/etc. etc.?

Can't they tell?

Well, obviously not.

So what's the answer?

Can I suggest - communication.

Yes, it may just be as simple as that.

Try sitting down with your family/partner/whoever and tell the truth. Something like the following:

> *'Look, sometimes when I get home I feel really drained/tired/exhausted from a hard day's work/journey/driving/etc. Sometimes I feel really stressed out from all the nonsense/whatever at work. When I feel like this it is very difficult to arrive home and immediately engage with the family. I need a timeout for 5/10/15 minutes so that I can relax/unwind/chill out. It will be for all our benefits because when I have finished I will be the person you have grown to know and love rather than some zombie who has walked in from another planet'.*

Perhaps some of you are thinking that this sort of attitude is rather selfish or disloyal.

I think not. All you are asking for is a little rest between the rat race of work and the rat race that can be home life. And even Olympic athletes take a 5 minute breather between races!
So it is quite normal to catch your breath between tasks.

The point is that this personal quality time helps you to recharge your batteries and mentally change from work to domestic mode. You may have to change roles from a lowly employee to the head of a large family – or in my case the head of a company to the guy who takes out the trash!

What you do to take 'time out' and switch from work to family mode depends on you. One friend, who does a physical job, gets out of his work clothes and showers when he gets home. He literally washes his work cares away and changes his attitude with his clothes from a corporate uniform to relaxed casual clothes.

Another friend, who has a mundane and repetitive job, exiles his family to the living room whilst he creates in the kitchen. He emerges mentally recharged, and to his wife's delight, with food. The family then talk about their day over the meal.

> *What you do to take 'time out' and switch from work to family mode depends on you.*

It does not matter what trick you use to grab some breathing space and change mode from work to home so long as it works for you (and if you do have a family - it does not take all evening!). Keeping this time for You works wonders. For I learnt a little fact a long time ago and that is you should never give 100% of yourself to any relationship, be it your family, work, hobby, whatever. You should always hold back 10% to 20% for yourself.

I can just hear lots of you thinking 'What a terrible thing to say'.
Well – no – just think about it a little.

You're not planning for the relationship to break down; in fact you are doing everything you can to make sure it is totally successful.
But say it doesn't last for whatever reason, and you've put in 100%. How are you going to feel? How are you going to be?
Devastated, might be a good description, and what have you got to fall back on to help you get through this crisis. Well, nothing, because you have given it 100%.

Compare that scenario with this one:

You have the same relationship as we discussed above and you are doing all you can to make it successful – but now, you make sure that you always keep some time for yourself. It may not be much; everyone is different. A little as five minutes a day, or maybe half an hour – you must decide.

But that time should be important to you. It is your chance to relax, chill out, unwind, whatever. You are building a secure foundation so you can support your family. And you are doing it with full approval.

And with recharged/full batteries you have more energy to put into your relationship. In other words the 80% that you are now putting into your relationship is worth more than the 100% that you were putting in before. And you've still got something in reserve. This reserve you can call upon when the going gets really tough: sudden illness, redundancy etc. You can call on it to become a strength for the family.

I hope that you now agree with me that a 'Time Out' is not such a bad idea after all.

Putting You in the Picture

- *Communicate.*

- *Take a 'Time Out'.*

- *Switch from work mode to family mode.*

- *Always hold back 10% to 20% for yourself.*

- *Recharged batteries give you more energy for your relationships i.e. 80% is worth more than 100% and there's always something in reserve.*

Another example of 'Less = More'.

Chapter 14
Are You a Couch Potato?

Develop Your Six-Pack as You Consume Your Six-Pack!

'Couch Potato' is a phrase that is in common parlance these days but what does it actually mean? My in-depth research department found the following explanations.

1. What mum finds under the sofa after the kids eat dinner!

2. Slang phrase to describe someone who watches many hours of TV, on a couch, and does not have an active lifestyle.

Let's just say:

A person who spends a lot of time sitting on a couch, usually watching TV, and not having a particularly active lifestyle.

I did wonder where the phrase 'Couch Potato' actually came from. I only knew that it was an American slang expression – but why 'Couch Potato'? Why not 'Couch Cucumber' or 'Couch Brussels Sprouts'?
Apparently, the expression 'Couch Potato' was trademarked in the US in July 1976 by cartoonist Robert Armstrong. Mr Armstrong, I understand, still spreads the Couch Potato Gospel.
His quote: 'We feel that watching TV is an indigenous American form of meditation. We call it – transcendental vegetation'!

Anyway - enough of that!

I have to admit that at times I can be a bit of a couch potato.
Let's be honest. Sometimes after a hard day's work isn't it very inviting to just stretch out on the settee, in front of a nice warm fire (unless you live in the tropics!) watching TV for a few hours, with perhaps a drink in your hand and a few snacks to eat? And, anyway, what's the harm? Well, none – if you only do it moderately.

Couch potatoes can do it all the time (so I am reliably informed) – even during the day. They sit there for hours on end staring at the TV and horror of horrors that's not all! Many of them will fully stock themselves up with all sorts of goodies to eat and drink. To make it even worse you can almost guarantee that the 'goodies' are all the things that should only be consumed 'in moderation'!
Anyway, they spend all this time watching whatever, and filling their faces with whatever. Eventually, exhausted from all their hours of non-activity they haul themselves upstairs to bed for a good rest!

My purpose here is not to give you some long boring sermon about the dangers of a couch potato lifestyle and list all the reasons why you shouldn't do what you're doing and that you need to be doing this and that instead. If you've got this far into the book then maybe you are actually considering some changes to improve your lifestyle. It's up to you to decide what.

All I propose to do is suggest that when you are 'Couch Potatoing' there are some useful things that you should consider and some things that you can do.

The Couch – If you consider that sitting or lying on a couch/settee/sofa/bed is the lifestyle for you then at least ponder this:

Is your couch etc. giving your body sufficient support? Many settees these days are designed to appeal to us aesthetically and may appear to be comfortable – but are they? Visualise this – you and the family are in a furniture showroom looking at ranges of different couches on show. You all sink into one couch after another. Each one seems to become progressively more comfortable than the one before. 'This one is really comfortable'. 'Yes, but try this one it's even more comfortable'. And so you go on until you find one that everyone and your credit card like.

Just consider this before you part with your well earned money. The more you sink into your settee/couch the less likely it is providing good support for your body. And furthermore, that sort of product will probably wear out quicker as all the foam or other forms of filler is constantly flattened, hour after hour, from the weight of Mr and Mrs Couch Potato.

Please don't think that I am some sort of killjoy puritan. I'm not suggesting that you buy a wooden church pew, but just be aware that good body support from your settee will protect you from many muscular and skeletal problems. If you also use cushions then fine - Just make sure that they adequately support the part of your anatomy that they are aimed at. Consider couches like beds. Most of us will know the importance of having a mattress that is firm enough to give our bodies good support.

Be honest with yourself – now, be honest with yourself. You've been sitting or lying on your couch for a few hours watching TV, maybe reading, or even listening to music. You now intend to get up. Do you need a crane or a hoist to help you drag yourself to your feet? Are you aching from various parts of your anatomy? Do your limbs feel stiff? Have various parts of your anatomy 'gone to sleep'?

The honest answer to some or all of these answers is 'Yes'. How do I know? Well, I'm human too and it's all happened to me. But I can give you a few simple ideas to alleviate these symptoms. I don't want to sound over dramatic – but. If you allow these sort of symptoms to continue hour after hour, week after week and year after year, then your body will eventually develop chronic conditions that will affect your health and fitness.

Now some of these symptoms may be caused by the poor support from your couch – already discussed. But they will definitely be caused by your body's inactivity. So what's the answer?
Well, in another part of the book I have advised the importance of stopping what you are doing, standing up, and giving yourself a good gentle all over body stretch every hour or so. (The AM/PM/Anytime Workout) The same applies here.

However, I appreciate that for dyed in the wool couch potatoes standing up is not an option! So here is the alternative.

Remember the 'Bedstretcher Work Out' – is there any reason why you can't use it as you are stretched out on your couch? You can even continue to watch your TV.

Depending on the logistics of your couch you may have to adapt the movements slightly but that should not be a problem for you. You will find that as long as you give your various muscles and limbs some regular movement and gentle stretching the majority of the symptoms to which I referred to will disappear.

It sounds so easy – but it is true. How many of us will admit to having lain on a couch for hours on end? We get into a particular position, we surely become more and more stiff, our muscles start to ache more and more; we know that if we try to change position we will suffer pain – yet we do nothing! It's as if we are wearing a straight jacket. Sooner or later we will have to move – but it's like going to the dentist – we know we are going to suffer so we keep on putting it off. When we eventually do move we suffer much more than was necessary. Aren't we mad!

Can you be a Couch Potato without a couch? Well, actually 'Yes'.
It's time to own up! I am no longer a couch potato, not even a part-time one any more.

I am now a 'Floor Potato'.

After years of practice I realised that sitting and lying on a couch for any period of time, even a good couch, was no good for me.

When I am relaxing I now spend a lot of my time sitting on the floor. You should try it; it is so much better for you. But beware, it takes practice. By that, I mean that you will have to get used to it and build up your floor potato stamina slowly. If you are a long standing (pun) couch potato it will take you some time to get used to sitting on the floor.

The basic position I adopt when I am watching TV or reading is as follows – The first thing I do is to ensure that I give good support to my back. I place one, two or three cushions against the couch base, sit on the floor and then rest my back on the cushions. I will stretch my legs out in front of me or I will move them to the side, I will sit cross-legged, whatever feels most comfortable. I sometimes try a part lotus position but not for long! Naturally, I will be changing my position from time to time.

Next position – for full relaxation I lie flat on my back on the floor. I use some cushions to make my head comfortable. The natural support of the floor will slowly and surely allow all your muscles to really relax. Just lying on the floor is a really good way to relax and get rid of all that tension out of your body. If you position yourself carefully, you can still watch TV!

Advantages – the floor gives us a natural firm support for our body. The cushions provide the soft comfortable feeling we desire. We are in a good position to carry out stretching workouts.

Couch Potato Workout – if you now go to The Tool Box you can follow the Couch Potato Workout. In the Tool Box I describe two workouts, one on the couch and one on the floor. It will work on the couch, but try it on the floor it's so much better. Go on!

Aching Backs and Relaxation – most couch potatoes will suffer with aching backs at some time or other. It just goes with the territory. Lying flat on the floor when you have an aching back is actually one of the best things you can do. Why? Because it is one of the best positions to really allow all the muscles to fully relax. Allowing the muscles to fully relax will speed up the recovery process.

Even better way – I've found an even better way to help aching backs. I've used this myself and told countless numbers of people to try it.

Get yourself a chair or a stool. Lie flat on your back on the floor, bend your legs at the hips and knees at 90-degree angles and then rest your calves on the chair seat. Practise so that the height of the chair seat is correct to give you those 90-degree angles. You can always use cushions or books or something to get the height right. Place your arms by your sides, breathe gently in and out allowing your stomach to rise and fall (abdominal breathing). Ensure that you relax your shoulders. You should find this an even more relaxing position than just lying flat on the floor. Do it for as long as you like whenever you like (minimum of 15 minutes is best). It's a great way to relax or just unwind. It will really help you to heal your aching backs.

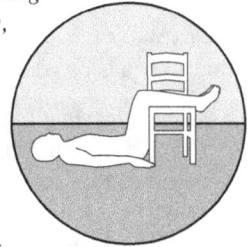

'Develop your six-pack as you consume your six-pack'! At last! You've been reading the whole chapter wondering if he was ever going to refer to the 'Six-Pack' bit. Well now is the moment.

OK. I own up. It's a joke really just to catch your attention – but not quite.

By definition, if you are a couch potato you will be more interested in consuming your six-pack. You won't be interested in developing it!

Still, let's assume that this book is the first thing that has ever encouraged you to do something to change your lifestyle for the better. Fantastic!

Here's a simple little exercise that is easy to do and according to scientific experts is one of the more effective ways to strengthen and develop your abdominal muscles (six-pack).

For the record, we should assume that if you have a beer belly or are otherwise overweight in the stomach department then you would also be considering some appropriate changes to your diet!

The Cycling Workout – lie flat on your back (See – even couch potatoes can do this workout).

> *Press your lower back into the floor, and then raise your knees to about a 45-degree angle. Place your hands behind your head with your fingers interlaced. Rotate your legs as if you were cycling. Be careful not to twist or raise your back. Don't pull on your head or neck. Don't forget to breathe; don't hold your breath.* **See the Glossary.**

With all exercises, don't overdo it. Build up the number of leg movements gradually. I try to do this exercise most days and usually do about 60 to 70 pedals on each leg.

But it did take me some time to build up to this number. The interesting thing with this exercise is that, unlike a typical series of sit-ups I don't have any aching in my abdominal muscles. Mind you I did find that my thighs ached when I first started doing this little workout. So you finish your workout and relax on your back for a few moments and don't really feel like anything has happened to you. But as soon as you stand up you feel as if your abdominal muscles have been tightened up from the inside working out. It is a really good feeling.

Putting You in the Picture

Don't be a Couch Potato! But if you have to, then:

- *Ensure your couch is giving good support to your body.*
- *Stretch out regularly.*
- *Do the Couch Potato workout.*
- *Try it on the floor.*
- *Try being a Floor Potato.*
- *Try the aching back exercise – when you need to.*
- *Try the aching back exercise – it will help you avoid aching backs.*
- *Do the aching back exercise – just to relax.*
- *Try the cycling exercise – develop your six-pack!*

Chapter 15
Fitness Training

There is an ancient form of exercise that has been practised in the Far East for thousands of years and is also very popular in the west.

Learning this fitness regime takes a minimum of a year to grasp the basics and up to another ten to master. Equipment cost varies from country to country: it ranges from wildly expensive at over a month's wages to nothing.

Luckily the authors of this book have been using this fitness system for decades and are convinced that you could use this exercise regime that was also mastered by the likes of Bruce Lee, Muhammad Ali and Babe Ruth, to name but a few. This fitness regime, probably with the most participants in the world is...

WALKING!

Are you disappointed? Did you expect some obscure oriental way that gave you instant health? Well, don't knock walking – it took you long enough to learn it and the benefits far outweigh the effort you have to put in.

So let's study the how, when and where's and why's of walking and find out why it is a superb tool to gain and maintain fitness.

THE LOST ART

At the height of the Cold War the American government studied walking. They wanted to find the most economical method of using your legs so that their soldiers could move around the battlefield with the least amount of fatigue. And they found it. Unfortunately, if you are able to read this paragraph it is already too late for you to learn this economic walking – you have developed your own walking style. However there are tips and techniques you can apply to all walking from a quick trip to the shop for bread, a long distance hike or a shopping expedition to find the perfect shoes to go with that dress. (They're in the first shop!)

Walking upright is one of the things that define us as humans, along with using cutlery. Learning to walk is one of the few times in our lives when everyone praises you for doing something – until, as a toddler, you are into everything! Yet it has become a lost art – we walk from the house to the car, from the car park to the lift, from the lift to the desk.

Walking has become the preserve of old men exercising their dogs; the young, if they exercise at all, prefer to don tracksuits and jog – pounding their joints to pieces on the pavement. Yet this was not always so – the 'evening constitutional' was as much part of a dinner party as the soup. Most of Jane Austen's characters did their social jousting whilst walking and she would have been amazed that centuries later people are writing and reading about how to walk - that most basic of skills. Yet such is modern life. So let's have a look at how we walk.

THE MECHANICS OF WALKING

Walking consists of the following determinants: pelvic rotation, pelvic tilt, knee flex, foot mechanics, knee mechanics, and lateral pelvic displacement. With all that going on it's no wonder that kids take so long to learn to walk! But do not worry - none of these terms are of any use to us. If we start concentrating on where we point the foot, ensuring that our stride is 64.5% the length of our leg and that our left eyebrow is in the optimum position, we will not walk – we will fall over! The simplest way to improve your walking is to walk.

At slow speeds, dawdling around the shops, etc., not much goes on when we walk – you stick your leg forwards, your heel hits the ground, your centre of gravity moves over your forward leg and your back leg moves forward. And so on, and on and on... A relaxed movement with little obvious energy expenditure.

When the pace increases – rushing for the bus etc., you spend more energy as the rest of the body comes into play. Your hips swing to increase your stride length and your upper body counter-rotates to counteract the swing of your hips (you see this when you start to swing your arms). This upper body action means that not only does walking help your legs but also your biceps, stomach, chest and shoulders too.

Walking is what is known as an aerobic exercise – a 'with oxygen' exercise as the sports scientists call it. In other words you burn calories by increasing the load on muscles which in turn increases the oxygen you need (you breathe harder) and you burn more calories (sugar and fat).

WALK OR RUN?

Running is one sport that will get you fit – fast. But like participating in all top sports you need to be dedicated and to have dedicated equipment: top quality running shoes from a specialist shop. Before you part with your well-earned cash and a part of your life to the sport of running indulge me and take part in an experiment.

Take a stroll around your local park one Sunday morning and count how many people are out running. How many did you count? Ten? Twenty? You probably only met about two – the rest were jogging.

The difference between jogging and running is speed – and boy do these runners move. Joggers risk the same injuries to their joints as runners – the impact when the foot hits the floor is 4 to 5 times your body weight but with a fraction of the fitness benefits of running. In fact some joggers move not much faster than a brisk walker so they risk injury without much greater fitness benefit.

> *If you want to take up the sport of running, go for it. Join a club, get some advice on footwear and enjoy. For the rest of us, with too much to do in a day, or perhaps carrying too much around the middle, we recommend the gentle art of walking.*

If you want to take up the sport of running, go for it. Join a club, get some advice on footwear and enjoy. For the rest of us, with too much to do in a day, or perhaps carrying too much around the middle, we recommend the gentle art of walking.

HOW FAR

Outdoor pursuit shops sell pedometers – tiny devices, about the size of a matchbox, that you fix to your belt and count how many strides you take. When you start you enter the length of your stride and hey presto! It works out how far you have walked. We recommend you do not bother with one.

Nor do we tell you to get a map measurer and mark out a hilly course. The only thing we want you to use is a watch. Timing your walk avoids the pitfalls that many people find when they join a gym or follow a fitness regime. Setting yourself targets mean you can fail them – and that is one of the main reasons why people give up on the gym regime. They fail, get despondent, and they give up. Who can blame them? By following your watch rather than a gym instructor, and by adjusting your pace to suit yourself, you have a custom-made fitness programme without the expense of a personal trainer.

FINDING YOUR PACE

On the army parade ground the pace and stride length are set: 30-inch stride, 120 paces per minute. These are 'catch all' standards so the 6 foot 6 guardsman and the 5-foot female nurse can cross the parade ground together. This works for the parade ground but not for the walking that we want. You must find your own pace and stride that match your own level of fitness, length of leg and the terrain you are covering. Nothing is more tiring than walking at another's pace – be it dawdling around the shops with your wife or trying to catch up with your husband's long legs. Do not try to lengthen your stride artificially – relax and get into a rhythm. Once you have this rhythm, stick to it. Going up hill, shorten your pace but keep the same rhythm. This will allow you to relax, go further and enjoy your walk.

Do not try to lengthen your stride artificially – relax and get into a rhythm. Once you have this rhythm, stick to it. Going up hill, shorten your pace but keep the same rhythm. This will allow you to relax, go further and enjoy your walk.

HOW FAR AND HOW FAST?

No pain, no gain? No way! My motto is 'take it easy and take it slow'. If you cannot maintain a normal conversation with some one then you are going too fast. Listen to your own body, follow The Walking Tool in the Tool Box and fill in the feedback section. This will give you how far and how fast to go next time – and with our workout there will be a next time.

WHEN TO WALK

Unlike swimming, which ties you to pool opening times, you can walk anytime. But just keep your sensible head on if you walk at night or in foul weather. If you feel under the weather then try ten minutes of fresh air. If you feel that you cannot face the rest of your walk then give up and get home for a warm drink – if you don't tell anyone, we won't.

FINALLY

Getting into the habit of walking will improve the quality and length of your life. Once you get the habit you will find that it is an enjoyable and pain free way to fitness.

Putting You in the Picture

- Don't jog – either run or walk.
- The cost is negligible.
- All you need is a watch and some decent footwear.
- You are not restricted by opening times.
- You can do it anytime.
- It's THE enjoyable and pain free way to fitness.

Chapter 16
Why Can't I Get a Decent Night's Sleep?

Beating Insomnia

Let me ask you some questions:

- *Do you have difficulty in switching off and getting to sleep?*
- *Do you wake up in the night?*
- *Do you then have difficulty in getting back to sleep?*
- *Do you find yourself lying awake in bed, for what seems like hours on end?*
- *Do you wake up early in the morning?*
- *Do you wake up tired?*

It is more than likely that you will answer 'YES' to many of these questions. You are not alone; one in three of us will suffer with sleeping problems (insomnia) at some time in our lives.

However, there are many things that we can do to help ourselves.

The range of sleep we need is between 5 and 10 hours per night (the average being between 7 to 8 hours) – so you can see that there is a huge variation in what our individual needs may be.

Ask yourself some questions:

- *How much sleep are you getting at present?*
- *Do you wake up naturally before the alarm goes off?*
- *Do you wake up rested, or tired?*
- *Do you have good daytime energy?*

If you answer 'NO' to any of these questions then it is quite likely that you are not getting enough sleep – or possibly too much!

EXERCISE

This exercise will help you determine what your individual sleep requirement is.

1. Go to bed when you feel reasonably tired and write down the time. Don't switch on the alarm. Sleep until you wake up naturally. Write down the time when you are fully awake. How long did you sleep?

2. Repeat this exercise for a number of nights until you establish a regular pattern of sleeping and waking.

3. This regular number of hours slept is your natural sleep requirement.

BUT – what if your natural sleep requirement means that you wake up too late in the morning for your daily activities?

Dare I suggest - 'GO TO BED EARLIER!'

The wonders of modern technology – remember that old recording device of yours.

Well use it - and you will still be able to watch all those shows you must not miss on late night TV!

If you are not getting all the sleep that you need then it may be that you are suffering from chronic sleep deprivation. In case you didn't know – quality sleep is an important way of reducing STRESS. Chronically stressed people always suffer from fatigue and people who are tired find it much harder to cope with stressful situations.

On the other hand – you may find that you actually need to stay in bed for fewer hours. Aren't you the lucky one – your active lifespan has suddenly increased. Well, time soon to consider how to put it to good use...

The point is – we are all different. If I don't get my regular 8 hours a night I'm in a right state the next day; but my wife sails through life with bounding energy on 5 hours per night. Doesn't it just make you sick!

Now don't misunderstand me. I'm not suggesting that once you have established your natural sleep requirement that you must stick to it every night. Hermits may be able to but it is not realistic for us.

Let's be frank – we can all be social animals; we can all be dirty stop-outs with the best of them. What I am trying to say is that once the effect of your nocturnal habits starts to become apparent (fatigue, increased stress levels, etc., etc.) then you will know what your natural sleep requirement is to get you back on track.

Hibernation

Here's an interesting piece of information. If you try the sleep exercise test in the summer and then again in the winter you may get a different answer.

Apparently, during the cold dark winter nights most of us require more sleep. (Not just the fact that none of us wants to leave a toast warm bed to face a frosty morning.)

O.K. So we have now established how much sleep we need.

Now – what can we do to help ourselves get a good night's sleep?

Well – I'm glad you asked me that question – here are a few suggestions.

- *You won't get to sleep if you're not tired. So, despite what I've said previously, sometimes the thing to do is to stay up a bit later.*

- *Try to avoid catnaps during the day. If necessary take power naps (no more than 5-20 minutes, any longer and this will disturb your night time sleep).*

- *Try to take some exercise during the day, but give yourself at least two hours to wind down before you go to bed.*

- *Avoid stimulating drinks in the evening. The obvious ones are those that contain caffeine – tea, coffee, colas. You will also find that some cough medicines and herbal products contain caffeine.*

- *Try not to drink anything late in the evening, and empty your bladder before you go to bed.*

- *Avoid heavy or spicy meals within three hours before going to bed.*

- *Is your bedroom comfortable? Is the décor relaxing? Not too stuffy?*

- *Is your bedroom soundproofed from noisy neighbours, street noise, noise from within your house? Consider double glazing, heavy curtains, deep pile carpets, fitted furniture against 'offending walls'.*

- *More anti-noise suggestions. Ear plugs – especially useful to combat snoring partners.*

- *Room too light? Consider curtains with 'blackout lining', or use eye masks – or both. You should make every effort to make your room as dark as possible – the darker – the better.*

- *Are you warm enough? You shouldn't be too warm but you shouldn't be too cold! Consider hot water bottles, electric blankets, or a warm-blooded partner.*

- *Is your bed comfy or is it past it? Your mattress should be giving you good support, as should your pillows.*

- *Can you relax in bed? Listen to soothing music, read a book (boring ones are ideal – so this one would be no use!).*

- *Food. Don't go to bed hungry but don't have a meal late in the evening. Try a hot milky drink shortly before bed with a couple of cookies, if necessary.*

- *Try a warm bath before bed. Add some nice smelly herbal relaxing oils.*

- *Sex with your partner is a great way to end the day and relax into sleep. But remember - if one of you wants to and the other doesn't - neither of you will be relaxed! So work together on this (no pun intended).*

DON'T PANIC! The more that you worry about not sleeping the more stressed you will become. Remember that just resting in bed is doing you some good.
DON'T DESPAIR! I've got plenty more great suggestions that work - so carry on reading.

RELAXATION

A large number of us can't get off to sleep because there is just too much going on in our minds. We have had such a busy stressful day with so many things to think of and do that we just can't 'switch off'.

Here are some of my suggestions to switch off, clear your mind and prepare you for a good night's sleep. They all work, but find out which ones are best for you.

Suggestion One. To do when you are in bed.

How many times do you get into bed, switch off the light then settle down to go to sleep? And you can't! Why? Because your mind can't stop working. There are still a million thoughts buzzing about in your mind.

As soon as you deal with one thought – another one pops up – and so on!

TRY THIS:

From The Tool Box
The Mind Focus Tool with a small variation

Make yourself as comfortable and relaxed as you can in bed, switch off the light and then do the following:

> *Relax your shoulders and then the rest of your body as much as you can.*
> *Perform 'The Link' with your thumb and forefingers.*
> *Close your eyes and visualise that you are looking at a big TV Screen.*
> *Visualise that you switch on your TV but don't tune into a station.*
>
> *The screen is full of tiny black and white shapes constantly buzzing around the screen.*

These are all your thoughts buzzing around in your mind. Breathe in and out slowly and gently.

As you breathe in say to yourself: 'Switch off conscious thoughts'. Gently hold your breath for a count of about three. Then as you breathe out say 'Here'. Repeat this.

And then say on your in breath: 'Re-lax'. Hold for a count of three. And as you breathe out say 'He-ar'. Repeat this.

Then finally as you breathe in say 'Re-lax-ation'. Hold for three. And on the out breath say 'He-ar'. Repeat this.

Visualise that you are now looking at a totally blank screen on your TV. Your mind is now clear and you can relax into sleep.

If thoughts start to return - then repeat the exercise. Say it out loud if it helps you.

This simple method is very effective – but don't expect immediate results. You may have to practise it for a few nights before it eventually 'clicks in'.

Some of you may be lucky and find it works right away for you.

However – be patient – it's powerful and it will work.

You can use different words if you find them more appropriate – but stick to the basic idea.

Second Suggestion – to do before you get into bed.

From The Tool Box
'The Writing Tool'

Sit down somewhere comfortable with some blank sheets of paper and a pen. If it is a problem about the past – use the Stress Journal Tool. Write everything down that is on your mind or going round in your head. This is not an essay and nobody is going to mark it for correct spelling or grammar.

Nobody is going to see what you have written – so let rip! If you've had a lousy day – then say so. If people have caused you grief – say so. Call them every name under the sun if you want to. You will be amazed how good you will feel.

Write as much as you want; as many pages as you like. Whatever's bothering you – get it down on paper. It doesn't matter if you scrawl it onto the paper and it is illegible – because no one is going to read it. When you have finished – don't read what you have written. Just tear it all up and throw it in the bin. Go to bed and have a good night's sleep.

If the problems are a task you have to do in the future and it is worrying you use the planning tool.

Make lists and notes of all your thoughts for the coming days.

Break them down into the following:

- *Things to do.*
- *When to do them.*
- *Priority things to do.*
- *Not so important things to do.*
- *Unimportant, but still needs to be done.*

Write what you have to do and qualify them with some positive statements like those from the Mind Power Tools. For example:

I will pass the driving test tomorrow.

My interview will go well; I will get that job.

Recognise the fact that with a good night's sleep you have a better chance of gaining those goals. And these messages you are writing will reinforce a positive message into your sub-conscious. See below for more positive suggestions.

The writing tool is very effective to clear your mind and will help you to discard all your worries and stresses.

Third Suggestion

Many of us find that a good way to end the day and clear our minds and prepare ourselves for sleep is to say, or write, some AFFIRMATIONS and POSITIVE SUGGESTIONS.

Some examples are:

I feel completely relaxed in every situation.

I have a good and sound night's sleep.

I wake up feeling refreshed and ready to meet the next day's challenges.

Whatever problems (stresses) before me – I am in total control – and I always cope with them.

You can select or make up your own affirmations but:

DON'T BE NEGATIVE – for example:

'I want to stop feeling miserable and stressed'.

ALWAYS BE POSITIVE – for example;

'I feel pleasantly relaxed and calm in any situation'.

When you finish your session say, or write down:

'I am now calm and totally relaxed'.

Fourth Suggestion

GET A ROUTINE – if you follow the same routine for every night you go to bed your sub-conscious will think 'Oh – time for sleep' and sleep will come easier. Your routine may be:

- *Warm milk.*
- *Warm bath.*
- *Brush teeth.*
- *Half hour read.*
- *Sleep.*

The routine is up to you. Just remember that if the routine takes an hour then you will have to prepare for sleep an hour earlier. This will take a while for the routine and the suggestion of sleep to enter your sub-conscious and kick in. But stick with it.

All these suggestions we hope will put you on the road to a good night's sleep.

SO... SWEET DREAMS...

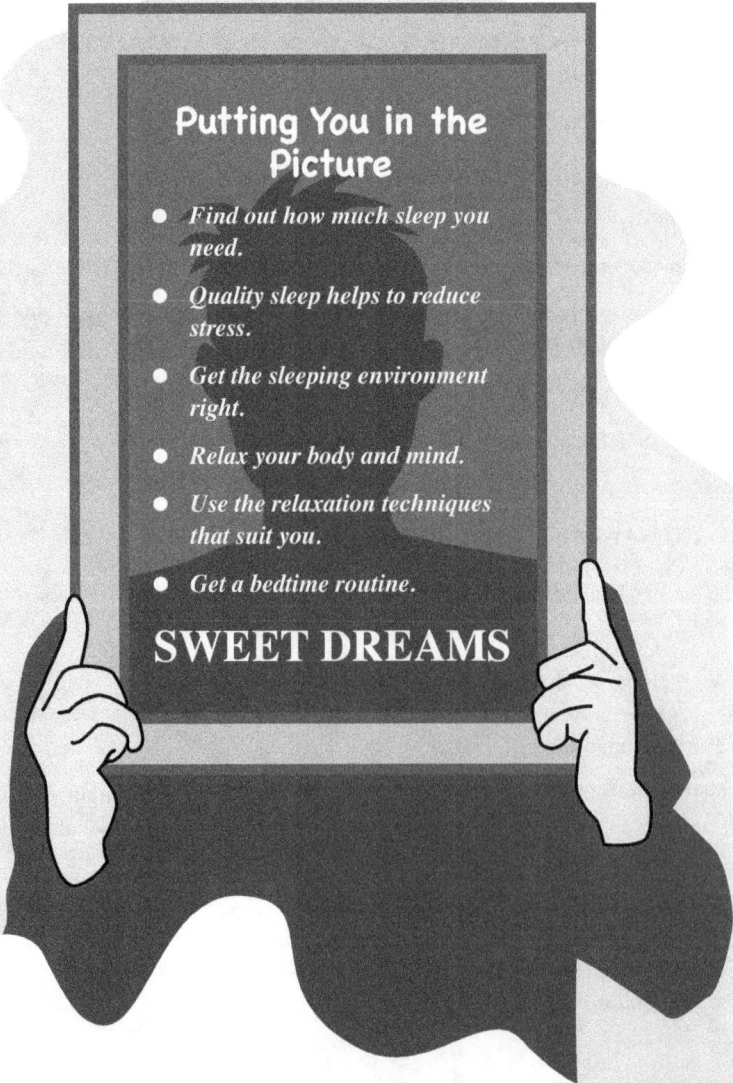

Putting You in the Picture

- *Find out how much sleep you need.*
- *Quality sleep helps to reduce stress.*
- *Get the sleeping environment right.*
- *Relax your body and mind.*
- *Use the relaxation techniques that suit you.*
- *Get a bedtime routine.*

SWEET DREAMS

PART III
The Tool Box

Chapter 17
Welcome to the Tool Box

Before we go any further let's make it quite clear that:

There is no Magic.

There is no Mystique.

I am not going to reveal to you the secrets of the Masters that have been passed down from generation to generation during the last two thousand years that have been revealed to me only, and I will now pass on to you for the trifling price of this book! Or any similar gobbledegook!

It will not be necessary to recite any special incantations or mantras when you practise our workouts.

It's down to earth common sense for us ordinary folk. And it's stuff that we believe you will find easy to do and you will enjoy doing.

There is only one secret and it's not really a secret – it's common sense – just practise.

Now Consider This:

> *'There are two mistakes one can make along the road to truth. Not going all the way, and not starting'.* (Buddha)

Or – put another way:

> *'The road to hell is paved with good intentions!'* (Dr Johnson and others)

In other words:

You have decided to take on a project. Let's say it's a project that will really make a big change to your life for the better. You are full of good intentions about the project and you want to do it. But beware – remember all those New Year resolutions that you made – how many did you actually see through! None? One? Two…..? It's not that your intentions are not sincere; it's just that you forget, events overtake you and so on…

OK – what I am getting at is that if you don't really intend to do something – don't start it. If you start it, make sure that you follow it through. If it's a big or long project then start off with small bite-sized chunks that you can easily manage that won't overwhelm you. As you complete each chunk you will grow in stature, confidence and awareness of your own ability to successfully do something.
If you start projects and don't complete them you are building up a history of failure. If you regularly start projects and don't finish them then your subconscious will begin to recognise this record of failure as your normal character. What chance will you ever have of achieving anything?

If you accept what I have said so far then it should be obvious that we should select projects that we think we will enjoy. Projects that we can easily manage that will not stress us out, with for example, continuous deadlines, diary dates or unreasonable demands placed upon us by either others or ourselves.

One thing is for sure. If we try to do something that we are not enjoying isn't it so much harder to concentrate and remain focused? Your body may be doing the mechanical bit of the project but where is your mind. Somewhere else – anywhere else!

Compare this with doing something you enjoy. You can easily concentrate your body and mind on what you are doing and you can see the progress that you are making. As you continue to progress so your confidence increases. You will be thinking to yourself 'I'm getting good at this – I'm really getting good at this. I'm really getting more and more benefit out of this' etc. etc.

It's too difficult!

Why do so many of us seem to have a very low boredom threshold? If we can't get instant results we switch off and move on to something else. However, there are some things where some patience is required. For example if you are learning to drive a car, play a piano, or practise a martial art don't expect to develop skills instantly. It will take time.

But every now and then you will suddenly be aware of arriving at a new level of skill. As that awareness hits you, you will think to yourself 'Wow' and a big smile of satisfaction will erupt over your face and you will feel a warm all over glow. Fantastic!

So – even if your project appears difficult or you don't get that instant result remember what I said – 'do it in bite-sized chunks'.

And then:

> *The first time you do it, you may think this is hard.*
> *But next time it won't be so hard.*
> *And each time it becomes easier.*
> *Eventually it becomes a habit.*
> *Finally your subconscious mind has it stored and it becomes automatic.*

I hope that you get the message that I have been trying to convey. We believe that all the Tools and Workouts in the Tool Box are enjoyable, easy to do and easy to master. You will notice the benefits from some of them immediately and some will take longer. Many of the benefits are more subtle; you may not immediately become aware of them but you will over time.
But please practise and give it some time.

Don't expect to change in five minutes!

Back to – just practise.

So what's really happening?

All you are actually doing is re-training and re-educating your mind (your sub-conscious) and your physical body to take on board some EASY ways for you BUSY people to achieve a FIT and STRESS-FREE life.

The more that you can practise the sooner your subconscious mind will start to accept these 'new instructions'. Then, whenever you carry out any of the workouts your subconscious will be working away for you automatically.

There is nothing special about what I have just said and it's not hard. Why? Well, you've been doing it all your life even if you didn't realise it. Just consider when you first learned potty training, riding a bike, playing an instrument or driving a car.

What made it happen? Well – just practise – and was it worth it? Of course it was, particularly the potty training!

What's so special about the Tools and Workouts is that they will help to transform your life – for the better – if you let them.

And once we have got over the initial trial period and we have started to practise regularly then they become part of our 'busy routine' and then it's easy-peasy.

So in order to help us all get through this initial period I will show you the simplest of little techniques or tricks that will help you along. In fact you will like these little techniques so much that you will continue to use them regularly.
We do – it's become part of us.

Attitude Check

I hope that you have now read sufficient of our book to understand that in order to become Picture of Health 'FIT' you only have to make ever so small alterations to your life. In other words you need to change your ATTITUDE to some things.

That's all it is – just small changes in your ATTITUDE.

So – when ever during your day you have completed a Tool or Workout just say to yourself 'ATTITUDE CHECK'.

That's all!

And what happens then?

Well, every time you mention these two little words to yourself it is reminding you and your subconscious about all the different tools that you are practising during your day and the benefits that you are earning from each Tool. And guess what – if you forget something – then 'Attitude Check' will pop up into your mind to remind you.

And – The Link (See Mind Focus Tool – Linking Body and Mind)

When you say to yourself 'Attitude Check' please do the following at the same time.

With each hand just allow the tips of your thumb and forefinger to touch together nice and gently. This gives you a good feeling of concentrating your body and mind together.

Two simple little tricks – but they work!

Some DOs and DON'Ts when you carry out a Tool or Workout.

DON'T:
- *start thinking what you will be having for dinner.*
- *start thinking about your shopping list.*
- *start thinking about a work project.*
- *let your mind wander.*
- *hold your breath.*

DO:
- *try and concentrate fully, in a relaxed manner (obviously) on what you are doing.*
- *try and relax all your physical muscles.*
- *breathe gently and easily.*

You will achieve 100% more.

Chapter 18a
Why Breathe? And How!

Everybody understands that we need to breathe regularly to stay alive. Thankfully, our breathing is semi-automatic: we can control it, hold our breath or pant if we want or we can forget about it and the body will take care of it for us.

The scientists call our breathing autopilot the autonomic nervous system. All we need to know is that it takes care of breathing for us whilst we concentrate on more important things like watching TV.

However, the autonomic nervous system does not control the way that we breathe. Maybe you are now thinking, 'How many ways are there to breathe? You breathe in – you breathe out – you use your nose or your mouth - and that's it!'

Well actually – no.

Most of us don't really breathe correctly. We breathe from our chests rather from our diaphragms - the bit between your breastbone and your belly. The effect of chest breathing is that we are only filling up the top part of our lungs with air/oxygen. Professional actors, singers and martial artists all use abdominal breathing. That way they use their lungs to the maximum effect and take in much more air: so they can project their voice better and absorb as much oxygen as they can.

Let's take a brief Ordinary Person's view into what is going on when we breathe.

During our in-breath we suck air into our lungs. The oxygen in contact with the lining of the lungs enters our bloodstream. But not all of air is oxygen – only about 20% – and the lungs only manage to take out about 4%. So when we breathe out we are literally blowing away 16% oxygen (that's why mouth to mouth resuscitation works). So it stands to reason that the more air we can get into our lungs, the bigger our 4% cut of oxygen will be.

Once in the bloodstream the oxygen circulates to our brain, our muscles and throughout our body. When it reaches the body's cells, oxygen changes to carbon dioxide which returns to the lungs and is exhaled with other waste products. So once again the more air we breathe in, the more air and rubbish we can breathe out.

So how can we increase the amount of air we breathe in? First let's see how the lungs work.

Our lungs do not have any muscles. They react to the change in the size of the chest cavity and to suck air into the lungs we have to make the chest cavity bigger.
We can make the sides bigger by moving the muscles between our ribs, or at the top with a neck muscle, or the easiest way, at the bottom, by moving our diaphragm.

To expand this area we adopt the following method of breathing:

Abdominal Breathing

Babies and children naturally breathe in this way, but as we get older, for various reasons, we forget this way of breathing. Perhaps it is because we spend so much time holding our bellies in! Abdominal breathing is done from our diaphragm muscle. As we inhale, this muscle contracts (flattens) creating a larger space for the lungs to expand and suck in air. When we exhale, the diaphragm relaxes (returns to its normal domed position) which allows the lungs to contract allowing the air/carbon dioxide to escape.

You can tell whether someone is breathing abdominally by watching his or her stomach. As they breathe in their stomach will rise with their chest. As they breathe out the stomach and chest will flatten. Breathing this way will ensure that you are not depriving yourself of half the oxygen that you could be inhaling.

I will show you how to breathe abdominally shortly, but first:

Let's have a look at the connection between breathing and our moods.

Our physical and emotional states are very much connected, with each affecting the other. For example your appetite can disappear if you are feeling down or in love, or if you have good news, the sort you cannot wait to tell someone, you are all full of nervous energy until you share your news. No surprise then that your physical and emotional states have a direct effect on your breathing.

For example, when we're stressed out or feeling nervous our breathing can become very short and shallow (chest breathing). If we are angry we can even hold our breath.

Most of us probably only use our lungs to their full potential when we laugh or cry deeply.

Can you remember an instance when a comedian made you laugh so much that you couldn't catch your breath and your sides started to ache? We probably all can – but can you also remember the feeling of relaxation that came over you afterwards?

Physical tension affects our breathing. Tension tends to affect us firstly in the usual places – neck, shoulders, chest, etc. – and our bodies tighten up. Then it affects your breathing – it becomes very short and shallow.

Compare this with your breathing when you are in a relaxed physical and mental state – moderate, slow, rhythmic and deep.

One of the simplest most effective habits to improve your health is deep breathing. Not only will you increase your oxygen intake but breathing deeply actually reduces stress - for just as a worried mind can influence our breathing so deep breathing can calm our mind. On the subconscious level we connect deep breathing with relaxation. It knows that when we are relaxed we breathe deeply. So the brain thinks that if we are breathing deeply we must be relaxed! Thus deep breathing, with our abdomen, will help to reduce tension, minor physical aches and pains, control stress and alleviate anxiety.

So – breathing abdominally allows us to open up our lungs to their maximum to enable us to deep breathe our way to becoming a Picture of Health.

Abdominal deep breathing is incorporated into many of the Tools in The Tool Box. But an additional tool, The Breathing Tool, is provided for you so that you can practise the basics. And – the good news is that it is easy to do – just follow our simple instructions.

Chapter 18b
The Breathing Tool

The fact that you have read this far through the book proves that you can breathe. But as with everything in life there is a good way of doing something and a bad way of doing something. Abdominal breathing is the right way to breathe - as we explained in the chapter Why Breathe? And How! It is also very straightforward. So simple in fact that you will probably laugh at how simple it is. Belly laughs we hope!

First thing we are going to do is test how you breathe.

THE BREATH TEST

Do not worry – this is not a test of how much alcohol you have drunk. And we will not ask you to breathe into a tube until your face goes purple. All we are going to do is test how you breathe normally. And this is how.

1. Lie down somewhere comfortable: on the bed, on the floor, or on the sofa. Place the palm of one hand on your abdomen – roughly on your belly button. Place the palm of the other hand on your chest – about where your breastbone is.

2. Now just relax. Do not concentrate on your breathing – just let it happen. Focus on your hands – feel them rise and fall with your breathing.

3. Once you are relaxed and breathing normally note which hand moves first when you inhale.

If the hand on your chest moves first, it is time to change the way you breathe so you can get the most out of the air around you.

If the hand on your belly moves first, it is a sign of abdominal breathing. Well done. Still follow the next few exercises to really improve the oxygen you take up.

THE BREATHING TOOL – HOW TO BREATHE ABDOMINALLY

To start this tool we are going to return to the same posture as we held in the Breath Test. By lying down we can concentrate on our breathing rather than our balance.

Before we continue with the tool, a few words of caution.

We all take breathing for granted – after all, if you can read this then chances are you have been breathing on your own for at least ten years! So when we start to concentrate on our breathing some of us get frustrated that we cannot master something we have been doing for decades. Do not worry – progress will come swiftly if you relax.

And even if you are someone who just cannot control their diaphragm as described, there are a very small percentage of people who cannot make themselves breathe abdominally, slow, deep breathing will always give a benefit.

Back to the exercise:

STAGE ONE – ABDOMINAL BREATHING

1. Lie down somewhere comfortable: on the bed, on the floor, or on the sofa. Place the palm of one hand on your abdomen – roughly on your belly button. Place the palm of the other hand on your chest – about where your breastbone is.

2. Exhale and let most of the air out of your lungs. Do not try to force the air out as if you were trying to inflate a beach ball. Just relax and let the lungs empty naturally through the mouth.

3. Now inhale through your nose, letting your stomach rise first. Imagine your stomach is filling with air, then your chest filling up later.

4. Exhale again through the mouth – letting your chest fall first then followed by your stomach. Exhale naturally.

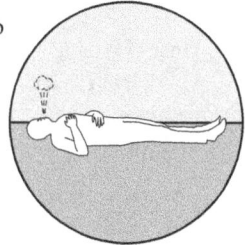

Once you have mastered this exercise so that you can perform five repetitions of abdominal breathing move on to stage two.

STAGE TWO – WE ADD SOME COUNTING

Now you have mastered the basics of abdominal breathing we add some counting to increase the amount you inhale and exhale and to slow your breathing rate.

1. Take up the start position lying down. Lie down somewhere comfortable: on the bed, on the floor, or on the sofa. Place the palm of one hand on your abdomen – roughly on your belly button. Place the palm of the other hand on your chest – about where your breastbone is.

2. Now when you inhale as you did in stage one, slowly count to 5. Make the in breath deep and long – imagine you are drawing all the air out of the room.

3. Pause for a moment, holding your breath.

4. Exhale to the count of 7. Remember you inhale more fresh air by exhaling more air out first. But do not force this air out – let it naturally flow out of you.

The emphasis on this stage is the long, deep breaths with that momentary pause between them. Once you can do 10 breaths move on to stage three.

STAGE THREE – MOVING AWAY FROM THE MECHANICS

Here we move away from the mechanics of abdominal breathing to concentrate on the mind. We assume that by now you can perform abdominal breathing and can slow your breathing without too much counting.

1. We are still lying down but this time place your hands wherever you want them - by your side, on your belly, wherever it is comfortable for you.

2. Perform the link as described in the Mind Focus Tool.

3. Inhale abdominally though your nose.

4. Once you have inhaled abdominally and paused, holding your breath, imagine your breath as a wave on the beach. Just as a wave breaks on the beach, rolls in, pauses, then rolls out again so imagine your breath flowing from your abdomen to the top of your head, pauses, and flows back to your abdomen.

5. Finally, as you exhale do not just let your breath leave your body but the stress and tension you have in your body too. As you relax rather than push your breath out stress and tension will flow out of your body.

Do not worry if you are one of those people who are not great at visualising things – you are still reaping loads of benefits with deep abdominal breathing.

This exercise is powerful not only to relax you but also to rid you of stress. However, it is not very helpful having this tool to improve your breathing if you have to lie down all the time. So Stage Four allows you to choose your own position.

STAGE FOUR – ABDOMINAL BREATHING ON THE MOVE

Obviously if we could only breathe lying down we would be bed ridden. We need to breathe through all our activities. So take time out to practice this in many situations.

Try –

Sitting – at the desk or watching TV.
Standing – this is especially good to beat the stress of queues!
Walking – a great way to improve cardio-vascular fitness.

But the real way to benefit from abdominal breathing is to add it to the Mind Tools in The Tool Box.

Good luck – and keep breathing!

Chapter 19
The 'Don't Panic!' Tool

Give yourself time to make a considered decision

BANG!

I do not know what caused it but stress has landed on you in a big heap.

It may be one big stress that has arrived in one big blow – a phone call or a letter with bad news.

Maybe it is just one last thing in an ocean of stress – something insignificant, the last straw that broke the camel's back.

Whatever stress has arrived, whatever caused it, it must be dealt with. Time for action.

You must do something – anything. It doesn't matter what. Don't just stand there DO something! Anything! It's better than doing nothing – right?

Wrong! Doing things wildly is panic and the aim of this tool is not to panic.

The Don't Panic Tool will stop you from making an impulsive action or reaction to a stressful event and allow you time, using other tools in the Tool Box, to come to a clear headed and reasoned solution to the stress in your life.

This four-point plan will short circuit your natural emotive reaction to stress. Follow it. Memorise it. Use it. Copy it into your wallet or purse. Following these points will stop the panic and keep you sane S-A-N-E:

1. **STOP**
2. **ACCEPT**
3. **NOTE**
4. **EXAMINE**

1. STOP

- Stop what you are doing. Your first reaction to the stress may have been the right one but was it? It certainly was not for the right reason. Kill the 'flight or fight' reaction to stress.

- Realise that wanting to immediately get rid of the pain caused by stress is natural – but getting rid of the pain will not necessarily get rid of the stress.

- Don't just push the stress somewhere else. For example – don't take it out on your wife because you have had a bad day at the office, or drown stress in alcohol. You are just pushing it away for a little while. It will return if not dealt with.

- Just because you are sad don't think you should make everyone else sad. You are making more stress for yourself and pushing away people who could help find the solution.

- Do not use terms like 'if only…' You cannot wish away stress. You must act reasonably to remove it from your life.

- Do not ask 'why me?'

2. ACCEPT

Accept that stress is going to make me feel bad. This is normal and if I did not feel this pain it would be very surprising. Ask myself 'how bad should I feel about this?' Do not try to deny or repress the pain but do not get the pain out of proportion.

3. NOTE

Note that even if this is the worst possible thing that could ever happen to me, the best way to deal with this is to develop a constructive, reasoned response to deal with the situation rather than some impulsive reaction.

4. EXAMINE

Examine the problem – if there is nothing productive I can do right now to help the situation then I must not dwell on the problem and reduce my morale. Check again: is there really nothing I can do right now? OK, then I will occupy myself with something distracting for the moment to keep up my mood and morale. Meanwhile, I will continue to stay calm and develop my clear head by practising the 'Mind Focus' tool and other tools. I will focus on the fact that a clear mind will give me the greatest chance to come up with the solution to my stress problem.

That's it.

This tool is designed to be short and sweet. In fact it is a little longer than we would like it. After all it is designed as a tool to stop you panicking. After all, you would not want the instructions on a fire extinguisher to go on for ever. You would be burned to a frazzle before you used it.

So here are the SANE points again. Cut it out and keep it with you.

THE DON'T PANIC TOOL
KEEP IT S-A-N-E

STOP

Your first reactions may be wrong. Stop them and stop loading the stress onto someone else or ignoring it.

ACCEPT

Accept that stress hurts. Do not deny the pain but get it in proportion.

NOTE

Note that the best way to deal with this is to develop a constructive, reasoned response to deal with the situation rather than some impulsive reaction.

EXAMINE

Examine the problem. Can you do something productive now? No? Then do something else to occupy the mind and keep up morale until you can think clearly enough to come up with a solution.

Chapter 20
The Mind Focus Tool

Develop 'Real Relaxation'

You can start on your path to becoming a Picture of Health by practising any of the Tools in the Tool Box – but this is the Core Tool that you should develop. In fact this is the key to success with all the other Tools.

This Mind Focus Tool will help you to develop Real Relaxation, 'unstressing' yourself and clearing your mind.

In fact, this tool concentrates on nothing but developing your skill at relaxation.

Once you grasp the basics you will find it very simple to do. In fact the Mind Focus Tool is so simple that many have laughed at it. But they soon stop laughing when they see how relaxing the Mind Focus Tool really is. After all, doing something complicated would hardly be relaxing, would it!

Once you have practised Mind Focus a few times on your own then you will find that you will be able to do it virtually anywhere, anyplace. I should add very quickly that it is obviously not suitable to do when concentration on a task is required. For example: driving a vehicle, cycling, handling machinery, etc.

You don't need any equipment to practise this tool. You don't need to light candles or incense, no worry beads to play with, and you don't need to learn any mantras or incantations. All you need is yourself.

When you have the Mind Focus Tool under your belt you can use it any time, any place and for as long or as short as you like. Anytime you need to blast away some stress.

But first the basics.

BASIC MIND FOCUS TOOL

The Setting

Find a quiet place without any distractions. This is only important when you start practising Mind Focus as it helps the beginner to have somewhere calm. Later you will be creating your own calm.

Place yourself in the most comfortable and relaxed position that you can, relax your body, relax your muscles, drop your shoulders. Close your eyes.

The Body

Breathe in and out – g e n t l y and s l o w l y – taking deeper breaths than normal. As you inhale through the nose, feel your stomach rise first, followed by your chest. (See 'Why Breathe? And How!').

Hold your breath gently for a brief count of 2. (If you suffer with breathing difficulties then shorten the hold to what is comfortable for you).

Exhale s l o w l y through your mouth, emptying your chest first and followed by your stomach.

Hold your breath again briefly and gently before you next inhale.

And so on… Repeat the above for as long as you like.

The Mind

As you breathe in and out try to clear your mind of any thoughts. If thoughts come back into your mind, as they will, then try and get rid of them. (Don't worry if you cannot get rid of your thoughts – as you do the workout more and more you will find it easier and easier to 'throwaway' your thoughts).

You will start to become more and more relaxed in body and mind the more you practice this. Soon you will begin to feel the benefits that Real Relaxation will give you.

When you hold your breath between inhaling and exhaling you are creating an emphasis, an underlining of your thought if you like. It's saying to your subconscious 'Take note – and Act'.

Linking Mind and Body

I mentioned in 'Welcome to the Tool Box' that when we practise any workouts we should concentrate our mind and body on what we are doing.

What we do with Mind Focus is 'The Link'.

THE LINK

With each hand allow the tips of your thumb and forefinger to touch – rather like a link in a chain.

In the early stages you can move your hands away from your body in time with your Out Breath. Then on your In Breath, semi-circle each hand (thumb and forefinger) towards your centre (two inches below your belly button).

The Link is not some piece of hocus pocus but a powerful way to produce a relaxing moment any time you want. In our simple Picture of Health way we will explain.

When you first practice Mind Focus your sub-conscious connects what you are doing with your hands (the link) with the feeling of mind and body relaxation. The more you practise this, the stronger the connection.

The sub-conscious makes connections like this all the time. Here is just one example:

Have you ever offered someone an alcoholic drink only to reply

'Oh, I got drunk on that once and now I cannot even stand the smell of it!'

I'm sure you're not the one who got drunk! Well, the subconscious of our drunk has linked the taste and smell of the drink with the feeling of drunkenness and the ill effects suffered.

In other words – smell of drink = memory of bad time. Drink = bad.

And the sub-conscious will reinforce this connection by physical effects too – people say 'it's turning my stomach!'

The Link does the same – it connects to the sub-conscious and that feeling of stress free calm that you created when you practised the Basic Mind Focus Tool. You will find that when you perform The Link your mind and body will move into a state of relaxation as the sub-conscious expects this.

Some of you, who are busy, busy, busy, always on the go and never really stopping until you collapse with exhaustion, may find the concept of really doing nothing a bit strange at first. In fact, when you first start practising Mind Focus you might find that you are dropping off to sleep! Don't worry if this happens to you – your body is obviously used to working full pelt and if it isn't, it assumes its sleep time. (Sub-conscious again) But keep at it, this sleep time will pass and Real Relaxation will take over. One tip, if you are dropping off to sleep when you start to practise Mind Focus put your alarm on for your allotted time – just until you get past this phase. This simplest of Tools will start to transform your life – if you let it – and guess what, you will actually find that you have more time available in which to be busy!

ADVANCED MIND FOCUS

With the basics under your belt you can really make this tool work for you. If you are strapped for time then you can give yourself a brief few minutes – which will give you a quick injection of 'unstress' and relaxation. If you have the time – give yourself the full treatment and let it last longer (about 20 minutes is fine).
You can do it standing up, sitting down, or lying down.

If you are on your own then close your eyes, if you wish. If strangers surround you then you may wish to do it with your eyes open. In this case try to relax your eyes, and soft focus on an object (not a person as it can really freak some people out!). Not only can you do it on your own but also you can even do it surrounded by people (e.g. standing in a crowded subway train).

In case you wonder how on earth you can practise this Tool in a crowded place let me briefly explain. As you develop this feeling of Real Relaxation you will also be developing your sense of awareness. So even in your crowded train when you are practising 'Mind Focus' and you have become really relaxed your subconscious will still be totally aware of what's going on around you. So don't worry – you won't miss your stop!

If you think that doing The Link in public will make you feel self conscious well don't worry. No one will notice you. But if you are worried then disguise the Link – carry a pen in your hand.

My favourite way to hide the Link is during meetings. I take my spectacles off and hold them by the arms. People think I'm mulling over what I'm going to say but really I'm getting calm and stress-less.

Mind Power Tools

Now that you're really getting into the Mind Focus Tool, start to look at the Mind Power Tools. By adding words and phrases to our Core Tool it really creates very powerful tools to use in unlimited situations.

Chapter 21
The Mind Power Tools

Unleash the power of your subconscious mind

The 'Mind Focus' tool is the simple core workout that helps you to develop Real Relaxation.

Now I will show you how to develop it into even more powerful tools that will help you deal with many of the situations that you are likely to experience in your daily life.

The Mind Power tools are the keys that will unchain the power of your subconscious mind. The tools will provide you with a simple structure that will enable you to feed your subconscious mind with positive thoughts and messages.

Let's start off by using as an example a problem that most of us suffer with from time to time.

A Cluttered Mind

How many times have you experienced that feeling of there being so many things going on in your mind that you sometimes think it is going to explode? You have experienced a 'stressful day'; there is too much happening, so many things to do, and your brain seems to be working overtime. You just can't 'switch it off' Your mind is cluttered up with thoughts and every time you try to clear them out something else seems to pop in. How many times has this happened to you, especially when you are lying in bed, trying to get to sleep?

Well, it's time that you started to educate that brain of yours to start behaving properly. And it couldn't be simpler – all we are going to do is to add words, positive statements, and positive affirmations to the 'Mind Focus' tool.

Once again, this workout can be done any time, anywhere. The same basic rules apply as I described in the Mind Focus tool explanation.

OK. Let's go.

Place yourself in the most comfortable and relaxed position that you can, relax your body, relax your muscles, drop your shoulders. If you are on your own then close your eyes if you wish. If strangers surround you then you may wish to do it with your eyes open. In this case try to relax your eyes and soft focus on an object if possible (not a person).

Perform 'The Link' joining your index finger and your thumb. This gives you more of a connection between your mind and your physical body then do the following:

With each hand allow the tips of your thumb and forefinger to touch. Then move your hands away from your body in time with your Out Breath. Then on your In Breath, semi-circle each hand (thumb and forefinger) towards your centre (two inches below your belly button). If you are in company and don't want to feel embarrassed then touch each thumb and forefinger and just make a small movement and imagine doing the full movement. It works – honest.

Breathe in and out – g e n t l y and s l o w l y – taking deeper breaths than normal. As you inhale, feel your stomach rise first, followed by your chest.

As you breathe in s l o w l y, say to yourself 'CLEAR CONSCIOUS THOUGHTS' Hold your breath for a brief count of 2. (If you suffer with breathing difficulties then shorten the hold to what is comfortable for you).

As you exhale through your mouth s l o w l y, say to yourself 'He-ar'.

Repeat 2 or 3 times.

Start to feel your mind calming, and all the clutter, hustle and bustle clearing away.

Now, as you breathe in say to yourself 'Re-lax'. Hold your breath again briefly as before. As you exhale say to yourself 'He-ar'.

Repeat 2 or 3 times.

Then as you breathe in say to yourself 'Re-lax-ation'. And as you exhale 'He-ar'.

Note: Try to spread the words and phrases over the length of your in breath or out breath.

Repeat 2 or 3 times

You will start to feel fully relaxed in both body and mind. Your mind will start to feel free from all the rubbish that was cluttering it before.

Repeat any of the above if thoughts start to clutter up your mind again.

Want proof that it works?

I have been practising this one for so long now that I barely have to do it at all! All I have to do is say to myself 'CCT' (Clear Conscious Thoughts). My subconscious reacts immediately and does it all!

Practice makes perfect!

A Variation on the Workout.

Here is a variation on the workout.

In this workout we add phrases on the Out Breath. Instead of just using the word 'Hear' we replace it with appropriate phrases that suit our particular workout.

Here is an example:

'The Re – Energise Yourself Workout'

Sometimes when I feel a bit weary and need a bit of a pick me up I will use this workout.

Instead of just doing the Mind Focus tool, I do the following:

On the In Breath I say 'Energy In'

And on the Out Breath I say 'Tiredness Out'

Or sometimes:

On the In Breath 'Relaxation In'

And on the Out Breath I say 'Stress/Tension Out'

I am not suggesting that you can use this workout as an alternative to sleep. But there are situations when sleep is neither possible nor necessary.

A typical example:

You have had an ample lunch with maybe a little alcohol! And then you sit down to a lecture/class/seminar and try to retain your concentration/stay awake. Hard isn't it?

Try this workout. I have used it many times and it works.

Conclusion

You've probably guessed by now that this workout is very flexible. As long as you stick to either of the two basic formats you can adopt them in many ways to fit your own specific needs.

Yes, you've probably guessed it as well – the more you practice your chosen workout the better it will work. As I have said before, there is no magic. You are only educating or re-educating your subconscious to react to your commands.

Lots of Other Situations

Now let me suggest lots of other situations where you can use the same workouts:

e.g. Before exams, interviews or important meetings – before a competition – before other major events – wedding, moving house, starting a new job.

Here are some words and phrases to start you off. These words and phrases are provided as a guide for you to play around with. They will give you a flavour of what you can do.

Once you get into the swing of it you will think of many others that will fit your particular challenge and suit your own personality.

Mind Power Tools will enable you to:

- *Develop relaxation.*
- *Motivate yourself to get 'Fit'.*
- *Develop your positive mental attitude.*
- *Boost your confidence.*
- *Increase your energy levels.*
- *Improve your concentration.*
- *Accept change as a challenge.*
- *Improve your memory.*
- *Eliminate stress.*

Words and phrases for many different situations

I am confident, I am sure, I am relaxed, I enjoy   exams/interviews/important meetings, they are easy, I remember easily, I am relaxed during exams/interviews/ important meetings, I look forward to exams/interviews/important meetings, I study well, I excel at exams etc.

Before competitions

I am strong, I am powerful, I have energy, I have stamina, I am enthusiastic, I am confident, I am the best, I can visualise winning performances, I perform perfectly, I am motivated, I am a winner.

Before other major events

I am totally in control, my concentration is 100%, my mind is as clear as a bell, I am totally relaxed, I am stress free, I am confident, I will succeed.

Wedding, moving house, starting a new job

My (event) is so exciting, I enjoy this major change, I am positive, change is exciting, I accept change, I am stress free, I can't wait to start.

Develop Relaxation

I am relaxed, I totally am in control, I am worry free, I am stress free, I am tension free, I am at peace, I am calm and relaxed, relaxation is my natural state.

Motivate yourself to get fit

I am fit, I like 'fit', 'fit' is healthy, I choose fit, I breathe deeply, my CV system is strong, I practise my tools daily.

Positive mental attitude

I am positive, I am capable, I can do anything, I like myself, I like others, others like me, I think positive, I act positively, my problems are challenges.

Boost your confidence

I am confident, I like myself, I exude confidence, I am capable, I am positive, I feel great, I am happy, I am liked by people, I am calm, I am totally in control.

Increase your energy levels

I feel great, I am full of energy, my mind is 'fit', my body is 'fit' energy flows through me, I am energy, every day my energy increases.

Improve memory

I have a powerful memory, I remember easily, I have a retentive memory, my memory works effortlessly, my mind is like a sponge, my memory is 100%, memory is natural.

Improve concentration

I think clearly, my mind thinks clearly, I focus easily, I concentrate easily, I concentrate effortlessly, concentration is natural, concentration is natural, my concentration is 100%.

Accept change as a challenge

I accept change, I enjoy change, change is a challenge not a problem, change grows me, change is an opportunity, I enjoy challenges, I relish challenges.

Eliminate stress

I am calm, I am relaxed, I am totally in control, I am stress free, I release stress, I release anxiety, I breathe deeply, I am at peace, stress free is my natural state.

Chapter 22
The Writing Tools

'The pen is mightier than the sword!'

We owe a huge debt of gratitude to the people who invented writing. It is a great tool for communicating new ideas, like the ones in this book. It is also a great way to relax a little by losing yourself in the pages of a good novel. Nothing new there, I hear you say but then that is you reading. I'm talking about you writing.

Writing is the most amazing tool for getting rid of your stress, your pent-up emotions and all those other bad feelings that have built up during your day, week, month or perhaps have been on your mind for years.

Writing is also an amazing tool for developing and planning your future. It's great to use as an additional tool to develop the power of your subconscious mind. Use it to reinforce the messages and instructions that you pass to your subconscious mind when using the Mind Power Tools. Definitely use it when you are planning projects or goal setting. Your project or goal may be just to go to the supermarket and actually buy the stuff that you need. How many of us have been shopping without making a list and returned home with stuff we don't need and forgotten the stuff we do need?

I'm not a scientist so I can not explain to you how the Writing Tools work; and even if I could there would be so much scientific or psychological gobbledegook that none of us would be any the wiser.

Let's put it into our 'ordinary guy', jargon-free, Picture of Health Clubs way. It appears that when the brain and the written word combine, it seems to have a tremendous positive effect in eliminating all the bad stuff from our subconscious, transforming our feelings of wellbeing, and conditioning our brain to carry out our wishes.

I know a successful psychologist who would often ask her patients to write down on paper everything that was on their minds; everything from the past to the present and their plans and concerns for the future. I can only tell you that she had the most amazing results.

So that's the background – now let's get straight into how we use the Writing Tools. We all must live in the present. Yet some of us live in the past – dwelling on past problems and it affects us in the here and now. Other people live in the future – creating plans and building castles in the air yet doing nothing in the here and now to get to their plans.

The Writing Tool helps both problems, and here's how.

THE STRESS JOURNAL – DUMP YOUR STRESS

People over the centuries have kept journals of their hopes, plans, thoughts and feelings. We are going to start a stress journal by writing down all the things that stress us out. How do we use this amazing tool to dump stress? Follow these simple guidelines and start dumping that stress:

- Sit down anywhere comfortable with some blank sheets of paper and a pen. Get a few sheets of paper – you do not want to run out when in full flow. Also use a sturdy ball-point rather than a fountain pen or pencil: it might get a little heated and you want the nib/point to last the session.

- Write everything down that is on your mind or going round in your head.

- Yes, write down everything.

- This is not an essay and nobody is going to mark it for correct spelling or grammar.

- Nobody is going to see what you have written – so let rip!

- If the thoughts come quicker than you can write – speed up your writing rather than slow down the downloading of stress. Use abbreviations, scrawl, scribble!

- If you have had a lousy day – then say so.

- If people have caused you grief – say so. Call them every name under the sun if you want to.

- You will be amazed how good you will feel.

- Write as much as you want; as many pages as you like. Whatever's on your mind – get it down on paper.

- It doesn't matter if your scrawl is illegible – because no one is going to read it.

- When you have finished – don't read what you have written. That's dwelling in the past again!

- Just tear it all up and throw it in the bin. Really rip your stress to shreds – scrunch it up into a tight ball and then throw it – and your stress away.

You can use this tool anywhere and at any time you like. Use it any time of the day if you are feeling stressed out or particularly fed up with someone or something.

I find that a good time to use the Stress Journal tool is before I go bed at night. It clears my head of all the rubbish thoughts and feelings that I have collected during the day.

Perhaps you are still unconvinced by the Stress Journal tool. Well you will never know until you try it, follow the advice above and really let rip with your stress. The first session may take you a while to complete – years or decades of stress may be waiting to come out. Or it may be that you are still a bit self conscious about putting all those thoughts on paper. Once you get into the habit of purging negative thoughts this way, the exercise will become easier and the benefits much greater.

THE PLANNING TOOL

With the Stress Journal Tool we were instructing our subconscious to dump all the rubbish we have been hoarding.

The Planning Tool is doing the opposite. We are now instructing our subconscious to listen to and obey our positive thinking instructions for the future. The future may be next year, tomorrow or even in five minutes time – but it's still the future.

This is what we do:

- Once again sit down comfortably with your pen and paper.

- Relax, try to clear your mind and concentrate on the Tool.

- If you are making a list for the supermarket – fine – carry on.

- Write down all your positive thoughts and instructions.

- If you are unsure what to write, start off with some of the words and phrases used in the Mind Power tools. Soon the words and phrases will flow.

- Go into as much detail as you like.

- Just remember to be positive. 'I will' not 'I want to be'.

- Keep what you have written – don't throw it away. You may want to read it again, to reinforce your message.

Example

Here's an example of some of the things that you might write in bed before you go to sleep.

'Tomorrow will be a great day. My mind will be as clear as bell. My concentration will be 100%.My energy levels will be high. I am totally in control of my stress. I will sleep like a baby and I will wake totally refreshed. I am totally in control of the project that I am working on/towards and I will succeed.'

Then – when you wake up in the morning you may wish to take a couple of minutes to reread what you have written to remind yourself and your subconscious of your instructions.

Once again, you can use this tool anywhere and at any time. Other obvious examples are before you go in for an exam, interview or important meeting – in fact for anything.

You may consider that the two writing tools are all so simple, and there's no cost involved, so they can't possibly work.

Remember the words from a song – 'The best things in life are free!'

Well taking control of Yourself can be free (except for the small cost of pen, paper and this book). It's just the high earners in the Stress and Fitness Industry who will try to tell you otherwise.

Go on – give it a go. Happy Writing!

Chapter 23
Inner Smile

Power of Positive Affirmations

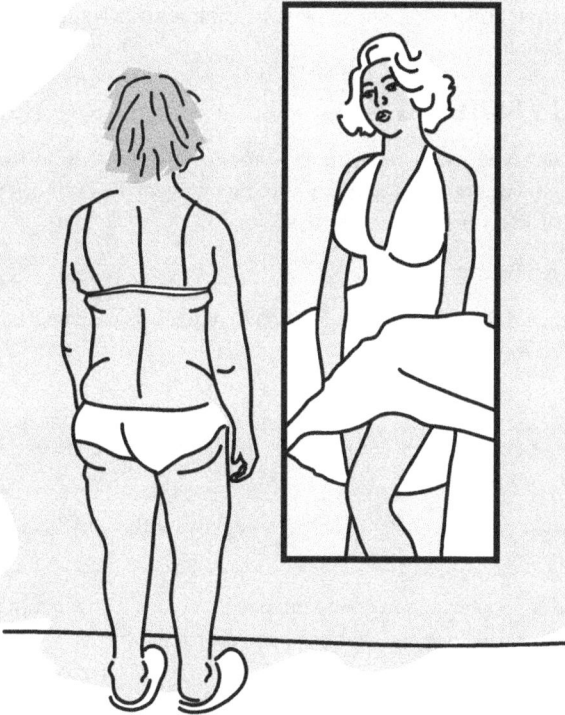

'Smile first thing in the morning.
Get it over with!'
W. C. Fields

Chinese philosophers (Taoists) say that we can't really love others until we can love ourselves. This is because we can only extend our energy of love when it overflows beyond the needs of our own bodies.

The stress of trying to give away too freely what you don't have enough of can cause blockages in your own energy systems.

Taoists practise an 'Inner Smile' meditation. With this meditation you get in touch with your inner self, and transform your negative feelings into positive energy. Following daily practice to master the technique, the effects will ultimately also influence people around you. In other words, once you learn to love (respect) yourself you will eventually have such an abundance of love that you will overflow with it.

Now don't get worried because I am not trying to persuade you to learn this Taoist meditation technique. Instead, I will show you a simple workout that will provide you with equal benefits.

FROWNING v SMILING

Did you know that you use twice as many muscles in your face to frown, than to smile? Walk down any street and count the number of FROWNERS and the number of SMILERS. I bet the FROWNERS win!

I wonder if it is a new exercise fad?

Have you ever heard the following expression? 'When he/she comes into a room it's like the whole room has lit up.'

I bet he/she was smiling!

Have you ever noticed the different reactions that you get from people when you frown and when you smile?

When you frown at people you are giving out negative vibes and what do you get back? Negative vibes.

When you smile at people you are giving out positive vibes. They in turn feel more comfortable in your presence and will respond accordingly.

Even people you don't know will react more favourably towards you. Smiling is a great 'icebreaker'.

SMILING AT YOURSELF

If you get a positive response from others when you smile, then how about –

'Smiling at Yourself'?

Don't you think that you will give yourself those same positive vibes!

How many of us ever really look at ourselves? I know that we probably look at ourselves when we wash or shave or groom ourselves – but do we really look at ourselves. I bet that for most of us looking at ourselves is purely job related. What I mean is that when we wash, shave or groom ourselves it is useful to actually see the part of one's anatomy that is being treated but that's the extent of it.

How many of us have been looking at ourselves just as 'job related'? And then one day we look in the mirror and for once really look at ourselves – and then shock horror:

Where did all that grey hair suddenly come from?
Where did all that hair suddenly go?
Where did all those wrinkles suddenly come from?
How have I suddenly aged overnight?
I don't recognise that person I see in the mirror!
I don't like that person in the mirror!

Sounds like some pretty good reasons to suddenly go into a big sulk or deep depression.

So – maybe we should get used to really looking at ourselves, really getting to know ourselves and giving ourselves a bit of loving.

It is natural to feel good when we receive praise and compliments from others. However, we are very busy people so let's not hang around waiting for this to happen; I suspect that for many of us we will be having a long wait!

Let's do it ourselves. We can praise ourselves, compliment ourselves, and feed our sub-conscious with positive thoughts very easily.

YOUR 'INNER SMILE' WORKOUT

Try doing this little workout each morning before you start your day (or any other time during the day that might suit you better).

Just take a little time out and really look at yourself in the mirror. Yes – I know – horrible isn't it! Especially if you haven't washed, shaved, or put your 'face' on.

But DO look in the mirror and give yourself a big SMILE.

As you practise this workout regularly you will become more comfortable with what you see. You will really get to know yourself, feel comfortable about smiling (to yourself and to others) and you will start to feel good about yourself.

As you look at yourself in the mirror say to yourself about three positive suggestions.

Here are some examples:

I am looking great – I am in total control – my concentration is 100% - I am totally positive – I can control my stress in all situations – I can do anything.

You will think of many others. Choose the ones that are most appropriate to you.

But remember – always speak positively.

'I AM in total control'.

NOT

'I WOULD LIKE TO BE in total control'.

After you have been through the affirmations finish off by saying to yourself:

'During this day my attitude will be one of – Smiling - Feeling Good - In control - Success, etc. etc.

If during the day I ever forget I will remember the magic words – ATTITUDE CHECK –it will always remind me of my Inner Smile'.

Practise this little work out regularly. You will soon notice that reactions from everyone around you will positively improve and you will start to feel much more positive about yourself and EVERYTHING.

Just remember the two little words 'ATTITUDE CHECK'.

Every time you mention these two words to yourself it will remind you of your little workout and your INNER SMILE.

Chapter 24
Why Stretch? And How!

Flexibility is King

In our chapter 'Fitness – Exercise' we discussed flexibility and the benefits of regular stretching routines. So remember:

The statement 'Use it or Lose it' definitely applies to muscles.

There is STRETCHING and there is S T R E T C H I N G. What am I saying? Well, to get the real lasting benefit you have to do it the right way.

So – what is the right way?

These are the rules for 'The right way'. It couldn't be easier.

Stretching

Well for starters we do not go through some regimented stretch routine where a sergeant major or an aerobics instructor is shouting out something like '1 –2 –3 – 4 - stretch, keep up at the back, Jones' or 'Come on – let's go for the burn'!

And – when we stretch – we do not just go through the physical mechanics of the movement with our minds wandering elsewhere. Picture one of those gym members plodding away on a treadmill or a bike or some other device, wearing earphones listening to whatever, or maybe just watching the big TV screen.

We focus totally, physically and mentally, on our stretch and r e l a x into the movement. Each stretch lasts for a good 20 seconds or so. 'Why?' You may ask. Well, the scientists have found that it takes a good 5 to 10 seconds for the muscle protection system to accept that what we are doing is safe, and then allow the muscle fibres to relax and change their length. Therefore, it is only after that first 5 to 10 seconds that your stretch really starts to do what it intended.

The Method – Tensing Up – Breathing

Are you one of those people who tense up and then hold their breath when they stretch? Well don't!

Just relax as much as you can and continue to breathe gently and deeply as you stretch. Gently stretch to a point where you feel some mild tension. Then hold that position until the tension lessens. If it does not, then ease off your stretch until you find a level of tension that is more comfortable.

Then allow the stretch to develop just a fraction further as you continue to relax and breathe.

This assists the circulation to the muscle tissues and assists the flow of nutrients to the muscle fibres.

Clothing

Whenever and wherever you do your stretching ensure if you can that your clothing is loose and will not restrict your movement. Ideally have nothing on your feet. If necessary wear socks. If you need to wear shoes etc. then try and wear a light pair of trainers. Obviously if you are at work or travelling this may not be possible, but try and loosen your belt and remove your shoes if you can.

Background

Background relaxing music is great if it is practical. It's a good way to really get in the right frame of mind.

Effort

Gently does it – especially if this is new to you or you are returning after a lay off.

'No Pain – No Gain'

Ignore this often-quoted statement. Do not work through pain. If you suffer pain, your body is trying to tell you something. Ease back. If in doubt consult your doctor.

The 70% Rule

Don't work flat out at 100% because you will probably work at 110% or more which can then result in injuries. Try working at about 70%. Then you can stretch without any worries.

If you don't worry – you will relax more. The more you relax – the more you reduce your stress levels – and the more you achieve.

By following these simple rules each stretch becomes more beneficial and rewarding and much more enjoyable. We obtain an immediate benefit and appreciate more fully the impact of our progress. We are re-energising not only our muscles but also all the functions of our body – both physical and mental.

Stretching is so easy and it's something that we should all be doing frequently during the course of our day. If you haven't got the message yet then try it and see what a dramatic difference it will make to your wellbeing. Why let cats have all the benefits?

All the stretches are in the Tool Box. Different programmes for different times of day and one for every time of day. Delve in to the Tool Box and have a play with them – you will find that stretching is not a strain.

Chapter 25
The Bedstretcher Workout

Start the Day Right!

You may want to practise this a few times before you put it into practice – concentrating on an exercise book through half closed eyes is not a good way to greet the day. Please refer to the Glossary for full details and diagrams.

Relax and Breathe

Just lie in your bed flat on your back with your arms clasped together on your stomach. Now relax, start to breathe in and out – slowly, deeply and gently.

Cat Stretch

Slowly raise your clasped hands up over your head and then gently stretch them and your arms out above your head and stretch out your legs at the same time. Do it again and give yourself a gentle all over stretch-out. Separate your hands and bring them back to the sides of your body by moving both arms in big semi-circles outwards and downwards.

Knee to Chest Stretch

Bend your legs so that the soles of both feet are sitting flat on the bed. Now with both hands hold the underneath of your right thigh just above the knee. Slowly pull the knee towards your chest. Feel a gentle stretch right from your hamstrings through your big bum muscles into your back muscles.
If you can, extend the stretch by raising your head towards the raised thigh.
Repeat the same stretch with your left leg.

Rocking Motion

Now using both hands, grip both legs, lift as before and then start to gently rock your whole body backwards and forwards.

Pelvic Raise

With your feet still flat on the bed and with your knees bent, keep your feet and shoulders still. Raise your pelvis into the air, continue breathing in and out, hold for about 15 seconds and then slowly lower.

Spinal Twist

With your feet still flat on the bed with your knees bent, stretch both arms out to each side and then drop your knees to your right side. This will give you a twisting stretch to your whole body. At the same time turn your head in the opposite direction to the dropped legs. If you want to extend this stretch, move your top leg further over to the right. Repeat on your left side.

It's as simple as that – but it's sufficient to get most of the night stiffness out of your body, and get you off to a great start for the day before you actually perform the next major task.

Getting out of bed!

Remember what I said about the safest way to get out of bed?

Well here it is again –

Lie adjacent to the side of the bed.

Turn on to your side facing the edge of the bed.

Pull both knees up towards your chest.

Swivel your feet over the edge of the bed to the floor.

At the same time raise yourself to the sitting position by gently pushing your upper body up with your hands.

You are now sitting on the edge of the bed in an upright position.

Arch your body forward slightly, place your feet on the floor and then raise yourself up by using your arms pushing down on the mattress.

You are now standing up out of bed without any strain or effort at all. Easy? And safe.

Tips reminder

All the stretches should be carried out very gently and very slowly. Give yourself as much time as you like with each stretch. About 25 to 30 seconds is best. Do not tense up or hold your breath whilst stretching.

Remember the 70% Rule. Only 70% of effort. You may want to remove some of the bed covers off you so that you can move your body easier.

P.S. At the end of the Bedstretcher Workout I like to do the Cycling Workout (it's in the Couch Potato Workout). I normally do about 25 on each leg; it's just enough for me to get the blood circulating. See what you think.

Now – Get out of bed and have a great day!

Chapter 26
'AM/PM/Anytime Workout'

Recharge your battery

As you've read my chapter 'During your day – is it time to hit the pause button?' then you will appreciate the importance of regularly stretching to ease out the stress and tension that is constantly building up in our body's muscles. Please refer to the Glossary for full details and diagrams.

It will only take a couple of minutes each time yet I cannot think of time better spent. Even the busiest of you can make time for this workout.

Ideally, you should do this workout every hour or so during the day. It's so easy to do that it will soon become second nature to you and then you will be doing it without even thinking about it.

OK – here we go:

Just follow these simple instructions

- *Slip off your footwear if you can.*
- *Standing, feet apart – about shoulder width.*
- *Knees slightly bent.*
- *Abdomen relaxed.*
- *Shoulders relaxed.*
- *Hands hanging gently by your sides.*
- *Breathe in and out gently two or three times just to help you relax.*

NOTE: Don't forget to breathe throughout the workout – don't hold your breath!

Clasped Hand Stretches (3)

Forwards

Interlace the fingers of your hands together in front of you at waist height.
Turn your clasped hands out in front and stretch your arms forward, drop your head forwards as you do it. Then return to your starting position. Allow the

stretch to develop for about 20 seconds and feel the tension oozing out of your muscles.

Upwards

Slowly raise your interlaced hands in front of you in an arc out and then up so that they end up above your head. As you do this movement you will be turning your interlaced hands outwards.

At the same time you will be pulling your head back so you can see your interlaced hands above you.

Give yourself a nice slow gentle stretch by pushing your hands upwards. Develop for about 20 seconds.

Backwards

Then unclasp your hands, move them out sideways and behind your back until they meet again.

Interlace your hands once again when they meet.

Now give yourself a nice slow gentle stretch by pushing your interlaced hands back as you open out your chest. Once again, develop for about 20 seconds.

Repeat the above sequence – if you wish.

Lower Body Jiggle

Find a wall. Face the wall and place your two hands flat on the wall at shoulder height, fingers pointing up the wall.

Now move both feet backwards a little so that you feel some of the weight of your body through your arms and hands. Your body is probably at an angle of about 30 degrees.

Lift your heels up and stand on tiptoe.

Now move from one foot to another by pushing each knee forward in turn. Do this a few times.

Jiggle your body weight about as you do it and you will get to every part of your system.

Feel all the tension escaping from your leg muscles and joints.

Limb Shaker

When you have finished give each leg a good shake in turn. Then shake each arm in turn. Then shake both hands at the same time. Shake away all that tension.

Finally

Neck Stretches (3)

Stretch out the muscles of the neck. This traditionally is an area where you always notice the tension building up in your body. You can do this standing or sitting.

To each side

Slowly turn your head to the right and feel those neck muscles stretch out. Don't forget to breathe!

Slowly turn your head back to the front and then repeat to the left side. Then bring your head slowly back to the front.

Upwards

Now gently raise your chin so you are looking at the ceiling.

Downwards

Slowly bring your chin back to the starting position. Now lower your chin down towards your chest. Then bring your chin back to the starting position.

Remember – it takes that brain of yours and your muscles a good 10 seconds or so to recognise that you're a friend and that it's safe to relax – so, hold each stretch for a good 20 seconds or so to achieve the maximum benefit.

That's it. Simple.

Do this workout regularly. You WILL feel instant benefits and you will be building up big credits for the future.

P.S. As you've gone to all this trouble why don't you finish off with a quick two minutes injection of 'Mind Focus' – you know it makes sense!

Chapter 27
Couch Potato Workout

Keep your six-pack flexible!

Here are two workouts. Please refer to the Glossary for full details and diagrams.

COUCH POTATO WORKOUT
The first workout is very similar to the Bedstretcher Workout for use on your couch/settee/sofa/bed.

FLOOR POTATO WORKOUT
The second workout is for your use when you have promoted yourself to a Floor Potato.

Tips:

- All the stretches should be carried out very gently and very slowly.

- Give yourself as much time as you like with each stretch. About 25 to 30 seconds is best.

- Do not tense up or hold your breath whilst stretching.

- Remember the 70% Rule.

COUCH POTATO WORKOUT

Relax and Breathe

Just lie on your couch etc, flat on your back with your arms clasped together on your stomach. Now relax, start to breathe deeply and gently.

Cat Stretch

Slowly raise your clasped hands up over your head and then gently stretch them and your arms out above your head and stretch out your legs at the same time. Do one at a time, two together, all together. Just give yourself a gentle all over stretch out. Separate your hands and bring them back to the sides of your body by moving both arms in big semi-circles outwards and downwards.

Knee to Chest Stretch

Bend your legs so that the soles of both feet are sitting on the couch.
Now with both hands hold the underneath of your right thigh just above the knee. Slowly pull the knee towards your chest. Feel a gentle stretch right from your hamstrings through your big bum muscles into your back muscles. If you can, extend the stretch by raising your head towards the raised thigh.
Repeat the same stretch with your left leg.

Rocking Motion

Now using both hands, grip both legs, lift as before and then start to gently rock your whole body backwards and forwards.

Pelvic Raise

With your feet still flat on the bed and with your knees bent, keep your feet and shoulders still.
Raise your pelvis in the air, continue breathing in and out, hold for about 15 seconds and then slowly lower.

Spinal twist

Ok, your feet are still flat on the couch with your knees bent.
Stretch both arms out to each side (if you can) and then drop your knees to your right side. This will give you a twisting stretch to your whole body. At the same time turn your head in the opposite direction to the dropped legs. If you want to extend this stretch, move your top leg further over to the right.
Repeat on your left side.

The Cycling Workout

Lie flat on your back (see – even couch potatoes can do this workout).
Press your lower back into the couch, then raise your knees to about a 45-degree angle.
Keep your arms by your sides with your palms pressed against the couch.
Rotate your legs as if you were cycling.
Be careful not to twist or raise your back.
Don't pull on your head or neck.
Don't forget to breathe; don't hold your breath.

With all exercises, don't overdo it. Build up the number of leg movements gradually. I try to do this exercise most days and usually do about 60 to 70 pedals on each leg.

Bear in mind that your choice of couch potato vehicle may have arms and backs that may obstruct some of the moves that I suggest. However, even couch potatoes will not find it too difficult to adapt my movements to their vehicle of choice.

FLOOR POTATO WORKOUT

Do exactly the same routine as in the Couch Potato workout.

But now you have more room so consider expanding the movements plus you can add:

THE PLANK - WORK YOUR ABS DURING THE ADS

The Plank, from the Strength Tool is a great way to build endurance in all your core muscles including the lower back.

Lie face down on the floor resting on your forearms, with your fists clenched flat on the floor.

Push off the floor and rise onto your toes, as you continue to rest on your forearms.

Aim to keep a straight line from your shoulders all the way down to your knees.

Aim not to raise your hips or let your body sag.

Try keeping your stomach, buttock and leg muscles tight during the workout.

Remember – keep breathing – DO NOT hold your breath.

Hold the position for a few seconds or as long as is comfortable – don't strain.

Try to hold it for one commercial - that's about 30 seconds. Try doing it during an annoying commercial - you know the ones, a maddening jingle or irritating salesman. Focus your frustration on your abs.

Chapter 28
The Strength Tool

How to become a man/woman of steel without pumping iron!

One of our definitions of fitness is to have strong muscles. This does not mean looking like Arnold Schwarzenegger and spending the majority of your life in the gym.

Let's look again at our definition of strength:

Good strength - your muscles are reasonably strong. For example, you can get up out of a low chair easily; you can walk up and down stairs without aching all over. You can carry reasonably heavy bags etc. without strain.

So average strength for average people. And to gain that we need an average workout.

No trips to the gym, no labouring under weight machines that look like they were designed by the Spanish Inquisition, no devoting a serious amount of your precious time to a gruelling work-out.

And no excuses. We ask for 15 minutes a day to build a body beautiful in the comfort of your own home, or workplace.

The work-out comprises of a starting warm-up and stretch, 5 simple exercises, and a cool down. All in 15 minutes. The exercises are designed for all levels of fitness and you improve at your own pace. No bellowing fitness instructor, no impossible targets, just you as your guide. Who is better to know your own body?

THE STARTING WARM UP and STRETCH

Arm Circling

Stand with your feet apart, about the width of your hips. Stretch your arms out above your head as if some one has pointed a gun at you and said 'Stick em up!' Now start to circle both arms like big windmills a few times in each direction. Breathe in and out with each swing. Do it gently and do not strain.

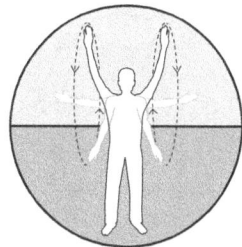

Playground Swings

Stand again with your feet apart about the width of your hips. Knees relaxed and arms hanging loose by your sides. Now, just by moving from your hips, twist your body to the right and then to the left and so on. As you twist in each direction allow your arms to swing freely with the movement, one in front of you and one behind you. As you loosen up allow your arms to increase the amount of swing. Keep your neck and shoulders as relaxed as you can. Continue for about a minute or two.

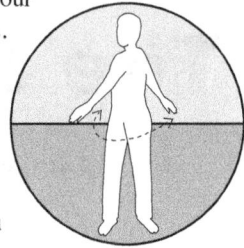

AM/PM/Anytime Workout

From this work out do the 3 Clasped Hand Stretches, the Lower Body Jiggle and the Limb Shaker.

THE EXERCISES

These low-impact exercises do not force you to deal with an unrealistic weight bolted onto a dumbbell or wired to a pulley. Nor will they isolate your Latissimus Dorsi muscle, wherever that is. Rather these work on your core muscles and your sense of balance, form and posture. Certainly more important than bulging biceps.

Each exercise has five levels. Choose the lowest level in each exercise and perform as many repetitions as you can. Once you have performed 10 reps of that exercise, move to the next level. It's that simple.

THE PRESS UP

Though we all worry about our waistline modern life neglects our upper body - arms, shoulders and chest. That is a worry for good upper body strength that maintains good posture.

POSITION. Hands shoulder distance apart, palms flat with fingers pointing outwards. Look forward, keep your body straight – this works the core muscles – and your elbows tucked in at your sides.
Exhale when pushing, inhale when you return.

Level 1 – Wall Push Off

Step back 2-3 feet from a wall. Place your hands against the wall at shoulder height. Lean into the wall, keeping your body straight and your arms extended. Your arms should be holding some of your weight. Now do the press up. Once you can do 10 move to the next level.

Level 2 – Waist High Push Off

Find a sturdy piece of furniture or ledge at about waist height. Take the push off position as described above. This time your weight is resting on your hands and balls of your feet. Aim for 10 reps and move on.

Level 3 – Knee-High Press Up

As above but using a bench, bed or sofa.

Level 4 – On Your Knees Press Up

This time you are on the floor and resting on your knees. Look slightly forward, and your upper body from your waist is now supported by your hands
Do the press up. You decide how far to lower your arms – do what is comfortable – no need to rush as it will improve as you build up your strength.

Level 5 – The Press Up

You are still on the floor. Look slightly forward, this time your body is suspended by your hands and the balls of your feet.
Do the press up. You decide how far to lower your arms – do what is comfortable – no need to rush as it will improve as you build up your strength.

LEG EXERCISES

These will build stronger legs. Whatever you do, never let your knees bend more than 90 degree.

Level 1 – Find a chair high enough so that your knees do not bend more than 90 degrees when you sit. A dining chair is usually better than a modern comfy armchair. With a table to support you slowly lower yourself into the chair. Once there stand up again. Do not collapse into the chair, the slower the movement the harder your muscles work. The table is there for support but try and let the legs do the work. Once you can manage 10, move on to the next level.

Level 2 – This time complete the exercise without the table as support. Get to 10 then move on.

Level 3 – This time we are going to stand at the back of the chair and use that as support. This means that the legs are constantly working rather than having a rest between effort.

Level 4 – Now we are going to use no support. Stretch arms out in front to act as a balance.

Level 5 – Rather than return to standing when you straighten your leg, go up onto your toes.

BACK LIFT

The aim of the exercise is to strengthen the back muscles. Lie on the floor face down with your body in a straight line and your arms by your side. The position of the arms in this exercise makes the exercise progressively more difficult. Always lift the shoulders not just the head as you can strain the neck.

Level 1 – Lift your shoulders off the floor. Do not give up if you do not move. Your muscles are still working. As they strengthen you will move. Aim for an inch lift. Once you get to 10, move to the next level.

Level 2 – Now add your feet. Lift both an inch off the floor. Keep the arms at your side. This will actually restrict your movement and stop you getting carried away.

Level 3 – Place your hands on your head. And lift the shoulders only. Now the range of movement can increase.

Level 4 – Add the legs. This is a really challenging exercise but we all know how important strong backs are. Get to ten and move on.

Level 5 – Place the arms out in front of you. This increases dramatically the weight you are moving but the benefits are great.

THE PLANK

Rather than traditional sit-ups that most ordinary folk struggle with we are going to use The Plank. It is a great way to build endurance in all your core muscles including the lower back.

Lie face down on the floor resting on your forearms, with your fists clenched flat on the floor.
Push off the floor and rise onto your toes, as you continue to rest on your forearms.
Aim to keep a straight line from your shoulders all the way down to your knees.
Aim not to raise your hips or let your body sag.
Try keeping your stomach, buttock and leg muscles tight during the workout
Remember – Keep breathing – DO NOT hold your breath.
Hold the position for a few seconds or as long as is comfortable – don't strain.

There are no real levels in this; just aim to extend the number of seconds that you can hold, and the number of repetitions that you are able to do.

COOL DOWN

The Cycling Workout – whilst you are on the floor.

Lie flat on your back.
Press your lower back into the floor, and then raise your knees to about a 45-degree angle.
Place your hands behind your head with your fingers interlaced.
Rotate your legs as if you were cycling.
Be careful not to twist or raise your back.
Don't pull on your head or neck.
Don't forget to breathe; don't hold your breath.
Build up the number of leg movements gradually to about 60 to 70 pedals on each leg.

Stand Up

And then from the AM/PM/Anytime Workout, do the 3 Clasped Hand Stretches, the Lower Body Jiggle and finally – The Limb Shaker.

That will do nicely thank you!

Please refer to the Glossary for full details and diagrams.

Chapter 29
The Walking Tool

The Best Exercise

WHY WALK?

Walking is probably the healthiest form of physical exercise.

You don't have to learn it – you already have!

You don't need any expensive equipment apart from a comfortable pair of shoes/trainers.

You can do it anywhere.

The likelihood of injury is low.

You can do it on your own or with friends and you don't need to make a reservation in advance. You can do it whenever it suits you.

You do as much as you can without straining or exerting yourself. Over a period of time your strength, stamina and energy levels will build up and you will comfortably be able to do more.

And you will feel – really good.

Tips:

- When you walk, land on your heel, roll through the foot and push off with the toes.

- Try swinging your arms and hips as you walk. This will help you to build up a sweat and burn off a few more calories.

- Look where you are going and don't look at the ground. First of all you won't walk into any lampposts! Secondly, you will actually take a longer stride and use some more energy.

Now let's get down to business and look at the following:

- Equipment.
- Warm up/cool down plan.
- Your personal walking plan.

EQUIPMENT

With 26 bones, 56 ligaments and 38 muscles and millions of years of development the human foot is the perfect device to aid balance, absorb shock and increase locomotion.

However very few of us have our own private strip of land free from people who drop litter, glass or forget their poop scoop. Nor do our loved ones wish us to attract strange glances by striding through our neighbourhood barefoot like some lost hippy. The only answer for us then is footwear.

FOOTWEAR

Your aim is for a pair of well-cushioned shoes that match your walking terrain. Opt for dedicated walking shoes, cross-trainers or hiking boots. The choice is yours but use your head and think of your feet – do you really need those top of the range 'Everest' expedition boots for a stroll around the park? I don't think so.

SOCKS

As we are forced to wear shoes or boots we have to have a layer between our shoes and our delicate feet. This layer – usually the sock – protects us from blisters caused by friction, gives extra padding and drains away sweat which keep our feet dry and our shoes fresher.

Walking socks, made from a natural material are best and are available from all good sports and outdoor leisure stores.

WARM-UP

When you start walking do not start off like an Olympic sprinter fresh out of the starting blocks. Allow your body to warm-up naturally. Build up the pace of your walking as you feel your body warming up and your joints and muscles loosening up. This is the best way.

COOL-DOWN

You should allow your body to cool-down as you near the end of your walk in a similar manner to warming up your body. During the last few minutes allow your pace to gradually slow right down to that of gentle relaxed walking. Cooling down your body this way will help to prevent muscle soreness and will give you a greater feeling of relaxation at the end of your Walking Workout.

YOUR PERSONAL FITNESS TRAINING PLAN (WALKING)

When you join a gym you want to get fit. A great idea. You wander in feeling a bit nervous and are met by a young, fit member of the staff who guides you through the payment plan, paperwork and privileges of the gym. Next is the tour where you are shown around the weights room where people are struggling on things that look more suited to the Spanish Inquisition than fitness training. Finally you are given a fitness plan that you are to follow. It looks a challenge but after all you are fired up with enthusiasm. But as the weeks go by the goals set for you seem as unattainable as when you first started. Plus you may have to put more time in work or with the family. Your visits to the gym fall away and then stop.
You are another gym casualty.

WHY OUR PLAN IS DIFFERENT

I do not know where you live. I do not know how fit you are or want to be, or how much time you have spare to get fit. I do know that there is only one important person in this equation – and that is you!

The four-week walking plan will not give you distances to measure, no taking of pulses or counting steps. All we are going to do is measure the time you are out walking and ask you how you feel. Easy.

HOW DO YOU FEEL?

That is the question we will ask you at the end of every walk. When you know the answer we want you to enter the results in the charts that appear later in the chapter. When you look back you can see that you have improved. Trust me, you will.

Asking someone how they feel will produce a rash of replies: 'great' 'good' 'not bad' 'don't ask!'. Hardly very scientific you may think! So we have produced a simple chart to gauge the effort you feel at the end of the walk. Your aim is to 'get a glow on'. You want to have an increased breathing rate, increased pulse, work up a little sweat. No gasping for breath needed just a warm feeling all over – a glow.

Once you have walked find how you feel on our exertion chart and enter the number on the walking programme. The numbers range from 1 to 7. Your aim is to stay at 4 – you 'got a glow on'. If the number is higher than 4 – ease up; if it is lower stride out. The great advantage with this technique is that you are your own judge – no targets to meet, no aiming for a mile in so many minutes. As long as you are honest with yourself this is the perfect training aid. Not only is it adjusting for when you are a bit off colour but as you get fitter you will need to exercise more to 'get a glow on' – and with no extra effort!

THE HOW DO YOU FEEL? CHART

EFFORT INDEX	HOW DO YOU FEEL?
1	WAS THAT IT?
2	LIKE A WALK IN THE PARK
3	FELT GOOD – COULD GIVE IT MORE
4	I GOT A GLOW ON
5	I'D CALL THAT HARD
6	I CANNOT CALL OUT
7	CALL ME AN AMBULANCE!

PACE

This programme gives you three pace speeds to meet when you train. Once again there is no calculating steps per minute rather a simple self assessment. Once you have warmed up try to maintain the pace throughout the walk – if you cannot, then just slow down until you feel you can speed up again. Here are the pace settings:

BRISK
The 'rush for the bus' type of walk.

MODERATE
Purposeful but not manic.

REST
Rest? One of the most important things in fitness training is allowing your body to recover. So take it easy – that's an order!

THE PLAN

Here are the charts – 4 weeks to a fitter you. Fill them in after every walk and when you start to give up half way through Week 2 look back at the previous week's chart. You will realise that you have improved. What's the comments and excuses column for? Well we all get put off by weather and life in general – be honest and try not to put more effort into your excuses than your walking!

WEEK 1

	PACE	TIME PLANNED (MINUTES)	ACTUAL TIME	HOW DID IT FEEL?	COMMENTS AND EXCUSES
DAY 1	MODERATE	20			
DAY 2	BRISK	20			
DAY 3	MODERATE	20			
DAY 4	BRISK	20			
DAY 5	REST	ZERO			
DAY 6	BRISK	20			
DAY 7	MODERATE	20			

WEEK 2

	PACE	TIME PLANNED (MINUTES)	ACTUAL TIME	HOW DID IT FEEL?	COMMENTS AND EXCUSES
DAY 8	BRISK	20-30			
DAY 9	MODERATE	20-30			
DAY 10	BRISK	20-30			
DAY 11	BRISK	20-30			
DAY 12	REST	ZERO			
DAY 13	MODERATE	20-30			
DAY 14	BRISK	20-30			

WEEK 3

	PACE	TIME PLANNED (MINUTES)	ACTUAL TIME	HOW DID IT FEEL?	COMMENTS AND EXCUSES
DAY 15	MODERATE	30-45			
DAY 16	BRISK	30-45			
DAY 17	MODERATE	30-45			
DAY 18	BRISK	30-45			
DAY 19	REST	ZERO			
DAY 20	BRISK	30-45			
DAY 21	BRISK	30-45			

WEEK 4

	PACE	TIME PLANNED (MINUTES)	ACTUAL TIME	HOW DID IT FEEL?	COMMENTS AND EXCUSES
DAY 22	MODERATE	45			
DAY 23	BRISK	45			
DAY 24	MODERATE	45			
DAY 25	BRISK	45			
DAY 26	REST	ZERO			
DAY 27	BRISK	45			
DAY 28	BRISK	45			

CONTINUANCE TRAINING

Once you have mastered this plan what next? The workouts will become progressively easier for you, and it will become harder to 'get a glow on'. After all you can only walk so fast until it becomes a jog. And that is a no-no!

- Extend the length of the walk.
- Add a hill.
- Change to more demanding terrain.

And most importantly, enjoy your new fitness. Reassess yourself by re-reading our definition of fitness in 'Fitness-Exercise' and make your own mind up on what's next.

Chapter 30
The Food Tool

We ARE What We Eat

Of all the Tools in the Tool Box, the Food Tool was the most difficult to create. In researching this part of the book we read hundreds of books and articles on food. Some have been insightful, others a bit weird, and others contradict each other.

The research into what we eat is vast and many commonly held beliefs about food are usually disproved, only to be re-established as facts later on. So anything highly technical on food can go out of date quite rapidly.

So how can we give you some simple, jargon free, Picture of Health Clubs advice on diet?

Well, let's start with some observations:-

1. Diet, to nutritionists, is the food we eat.

2. Diet, to normal people, is what you go on to lose weight.

3. Slim people do not diet; they just have some simple habits that keep them slim.

So rather than give you a list of forbidden foods and a strict menu to follow, we are going to give you some good eating habits to pick up. Like all good habits they take time to establish themselves. So be easy with yourself.

However, for those of you who have followed diets in the past and miss having rules to follow, here are three rules NEVER to be broken:

1. Do not follow the Food Tool as part of a New Year's resolution! How many times have you heard this story? You have spent the whole of December stocking up on goodies for Christmas – your home is overflowing. Less than a week later you decide, at New Year, not to eat any of it. So you either throw it all away – what a waste! - or you keep it the cupboard as a treat. It's not long before those forbidden foods start calling you from their hiding place – slowly chipping away at your resolve until you give in. Result: failure. So start the plan when you are free of any goodies bought for a feast. I would say buy less

in the run up, but we are only human. Similarly, do not start on a Monday – the weekend is an awful long way off.

2. You are not on a diet. We are not putting you on this strict plan for a few months until you get to your dream weight. Just as you picked up bad habits of eating from parents, your job or just being a bit lazy, now you are going to pick up good habits. Plus when your friends see the new you and ask what diet you are following, you can answer truthfully 'Oh, I'm not on a diet'.

3. Add one habit to your life a week. There are 9 habits, so that should make 9 weeks to a new you. But we are giving you 12 weeks – three weeks extra because we want you to pick up these habits and for them to stay for a lifetime. That's 3 months! Pick any one to start. People usually pick the easiest, it's human nature. There are no bad sacrifices to make – after all it is not a diet. If the habits look a bit strange on their own you would be right – each habit is connected to the other to make a whole eating plan. But like writing, you have to learn the letters before you can write the words. So plunge in – read all the habits and choose the one you think you can pick up first.

OUR GOOD EATING HABITS

1. IF YOU WANT TO GET THIN CLEAR YOUR PLATE! Or perhaps we should say 'clear your own plate!' It has always amazed me when I watch a family sitting down to a normal meal. All the family members, big and small, from dad down to grandma and the toddler all eat off the same sized plates. And even when we know the good advice of eat only until you are full it is human nature to eat everything that is put in front of you. The answer – everybody have plates to match their size. Generally I think the bowl of a dinner plate should be the span of a person's hand – the rim is not counted. Do not worry if you thing that you will be accused of starving your family – habit 2 will balance it out. And if someone posh is coming to tea you can still get out the matching set.

2. IF YOU WANT TO GET THIN EAT MORE! We are not talking quantity here – but frequency. Rather than having three big meals a day which may get you bloated and slow you down, we recommend eating many small meals. Eating 3 meals a day is a bit like a mini feast-famine problem we talked about in chapter 'Eating yes - Dieting No'. Eating three meals a day means that your blood sugar gets low, your body feels hungry and you eat more during the meal. Eating every 2-3 hours will banish any craving for bad snacks and when you do eat a meal it need only be a small one. This habit can take some planning to get right but you have a week to pick it up.

3. IF YOU WANT TO GET FIT HALT YOUR DRINKING! I know some of you
    have gone pale by the thought of no more alcohol, but I'm not talking about not
    drinking but the H.A.L.T. test. Never have a drink if you are:

    H ungry
    A lone
    L onely
    T ired

This just means you are replacing something else you need in your life (like food or
sleep) with booze. Now, how you apply these to your life is up to you. Personally
I believe you are never alone with a good book. But these habits can tell you what
sort of drinker you are. Try to stick to the maximum units per week - 14 for the
ladies and 21 for the men. Also try not to drink alcohol on two consecutive days
to give your body a rest.

4. CUT OUT SUGAR IT'S NOT COMPLICATED! Or to put it a better way,
    cut out all sugars, or to use the posh name, carbohydrates, IF they are not
    complicated. Do not worry .You will not need a chemistry degree to understand
    what we mean – a simple Picture of Health Cubs explanation follows.

Carbohydrates, like life, can come in two sorts – simple and complicated.
Something simple you can get straight away, complicated stuff takes a time
to work out. It's the same with carbohydrates – simple and your body gets the
energy straight away in one big hit; complicated and the body takes time to get
at all the sugar. Generally the more a food has been processed, like white sugar
you put in your coffee, the simpler the sugars it contains.

Have you heard of the popular GI index? It's roughly the same thing – the
higher the index, the simpler the sugar. Having a big sugar hit is like having a
big pay cheque, great I hear you say. What do you do with all that cash? You
spend what you can and what you cannot spend you save for next time. The
body does the same with a big sugar hit – it spends what it can and banks the
rest – but as fat. Complex carbohydrates give you a steady flow of the energy
you need without the excess to bank as fat. Plus you get the additional nutrients
in complex carbohydrates that were destroyed in the simplifying process. What
would you rather have to help you digest your food? Your body, nature's own
incinerator, or some guy in a food factory?

Whilst we are on the subject of factory food, we have to remember that the
people who make it have a vested interest in it tasting good. If it tastes good
you will buy it again. One way for it to taste good is to add sugar. But having
sugar high upon the list of ingredients can be a turn off to the health conscious

consumer. Also some ingredients are essentially sugars but called differently due to their origin or production processes – sucrose and glucose are an example of this.

So here we name and shame the simple sugars to be avoided which called by any other name still taste as sweet.

SUCROSE, MANNITOL, GLUCOSE, MALT, MALTOSE, MALT EXTRACT, HONEY, LACTOSE, SORBITOL, RICE SYRUP, RICE EXTRACT, MOLASSES, GOLDEN SYRUP, CORN SYRUP, INVERT SUGAR.

5. GET THIN BY EATING YOUR GREENS AND YOUR REDS, AND YOUR YELLOWS AND ORANGES. In other words variety is the spice of life. Most people eat the same sort of thing that they grew up on. It's safe food. Yet most supermarkets have a huge variety of choice of ingredients that can confuse even the most experienced kitchen warrior.

Explore the wonders of the fruit and veg departments, some of which display more tropical fruit that a trip up the Amazon. What you are aiming for is a splash of colour on your plate. Not just your meat, potatoes and a bit of green. Rather get as much colour on your plate as you can.

The more colour you have on the more chance you have of getting the different nutrients you need. Add to the fact it looks good (the first bite is with the eyes) Most importantly, there is a tendency to overeat when you eat the same food over and over. It is almost as if the body is looking for something it needs in quantity that it cannot find in quality. And a bored eater will soon start to eat the things they should not.

6. GET THIN – EAT BREAKFAST. Breakfast is by and far the most important meal of the day. When your body was asleep you were not eating. It stands to reason you should break your fast as soon as you can with good quality food. This will crank up your metabolic rate and you will start to burn more calories during the day.

The problem is that the food we usually eat for breakfast, the processed breakfast cereal, is usually no more than simple carbohydrates. You get an instant sugar hit then two hours later you are hungry again. And being hungry leaves you open to the temptation to have another sugary snack that will give you a quick hit only for you to be hungry again in another two hours.

The answer is to enjoy a breakfast that contains both protein and complex carbohydrates whilst avoiding the simple sugars found in most processed cereals. Protein can come in the form of eggs, nuts, yoghurt, kippers etc. Complex carbohydrates can come in the form of fruit (not too much dried fruit), muesli, porridge or even some left over veg from last night's supper. The choice is up to you, especially if you are not good in the morning and the idea of cooking is a dangerous one. The trick is to experiment and whatever you do, have breakfast.

7. IF YOU WANT TO GET THIN ON A DIET CHEAT! The main problem with diets is that you are given a list of foods that are forbidden and, being human, you want them all the more now you cannot have them. Even if you never ate them until you began the diet. That is why the Picture of Health Clubs Food Tool has no foods that are forbidden. In fact we want you to cheat a little. It is your reward for picking up good eating habits that are going to stay with you for the rest of your life.

   We believe in everything in moderation. So the question is how much cheating? We put it at 5:1. That is 5 good choices will give you 1 cheat. Because you are eating small meals during the day you will not feel hungry and give in to a sugary snack in a moment of weakness. Rather you can plan for your treat - the anticipation will make the treat even better.

   This means you can enjoy a full social life too. Rather than gloomily looking at the restaurant menu for the slimmer's option, you can enjoy yourself. Just remember not to go mad every day and stick to the 5:1 plan. My cheat is a glass of red wine and some very dark chocolate. Heaven!

8. GET FIT DRINK MORE. Before you reach for that six-pack of beer I have to tell you that it is water you need to drink. Water is an acquired taste but nothing beats the old H_2O to kill thirst. Putting it in your whisky or using it to make coffee does not work. Six large glasses of straight water a day is what you should aim for. The choice of bottled or tap water is your choice. Still, rather than sparkling, is easier to drink. There is a lot of gas in 6 large glasses. My own choice is tap water. And I carry a small bottle with me in and sip it whenever I need.

9. BE A GOOD PERSON AND OBEY THE CURFEW. We are not talking about you staying locked in doors from seven in the evening to prevent you from visiting the pizza restaurant. Rather we are going to stop you having certain foods at a certain time. Do not worry there are only two curfews to obey.

   CAFFEINE CURFEW. Basically caffeine is a stimulant that lasts for a few hours in the body. The last thing you need for a good night's sleep is a stimulant tearing about your body. So we are going to apply a caffeine curfew. Six hours before you go to bed knock the caffeine on the head. No coffee, tea, cola etc.

   Six hours is an average time – some people process caffeine more quickly than others, some more slowly. So change the time to suit you.

CARBOHYDRATE CURFEW. Carbohydrates are fuel. We need them to keep active. Being active will burn these carbohydrates. But when we sleep we are not burning very much in the way of carbohydrates so the body, not needing them, will turn them into fat. To avoid this we are going to have a carb curfew.

Dinner should contain no starchy food – potatoes, rice, bread etc. Rather you will have protein and vegetables. The complex carbohydrates in the veg will keep you going throughout the night until breakfast. But the carb curfew means no biscuits or cake in the evening.

When the curfew starts depends on when you go to bed. Once again the exact time is a personal thing. My personal time is six hours before I go to bed. I match it up with my caffeine curfew with my carb curfew – one less thing to remember. And I mark the curfew with a cup of good coffee and a chocolate biscuit!

For more motivation here are a few tips to help you to pick up our good eating habits.

OUR TIPS FOR HEALTHY EATING

Follow these simple tips and meals will be a piece of cake!

- Once you have worked out how much you need to lose – be it 5lb or 500lb – the minimum time it will take you is 6 months. Remember we are dieting not just to lose weight but to keep it off. If you have not reached your target weight in the 6 months but have lost some weight - give yourself another 6 months. And so on until you reach it.

- If you do feel hungry between meals have a drink of water. The body gives the same sensation for hunger as thirst. If you are still hungry, eat fruit.

- Eat at least two healthy snacks a day. Try fruit it's God's fast food.

- Eat moderately – don't overeat. I know many of us have been brought up to eat everything on our plates but once you feel full – don't shovel in any more! I know it is a waste of food but if you feel so strongly about wasting it – next time, cook less.

- Drink water with your meal. Even if you have wine, always have a glass of water available.

- Get into the habit of reading the Nutritional Facts labels to see what you are actually eating.

- Avoid low calorie diets. If you eat fewer than 1500 calories a day you can slow down your metabolism by 30% and leave you deficient in nutrients that you need for energy.

Chocolate is a danger food. Remove it from your house NOW! The best way to dispose of chocolate is to send it to me via the publisher. Especially that extra dark chocolate which goes wonderfully with red wine. OK, you got me. I love chocolate. Now I aim for quality rather than quantity and I use it as a reward for completing a nasty job or after a bit of exercise.

Remember we ARE what we eat – so happy eating!

Chapter 31
Glossary of Stretches and Strength Exercises

STRETCHES

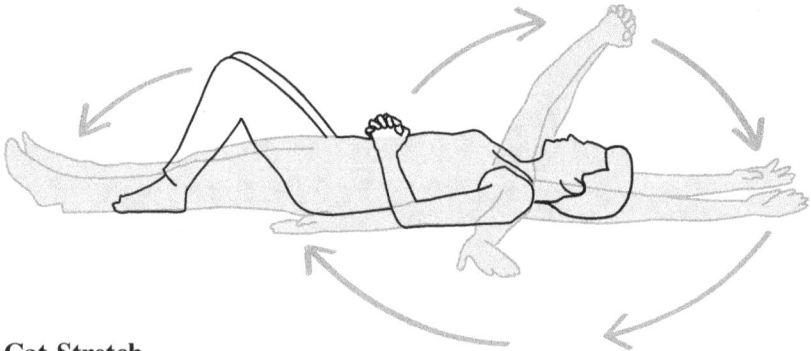

Cat-Stretch

On the floor or bed or coach, slowly raise your clasped hands up over your head and then gently stretch them and your arms out above your head and stretch out your legs at the same time. Do it again and give yourself a gentle all over stretch-out. Separate your hands and bring them back to the sides of your body by moving both arms in big semi-circles outwards and downwards.

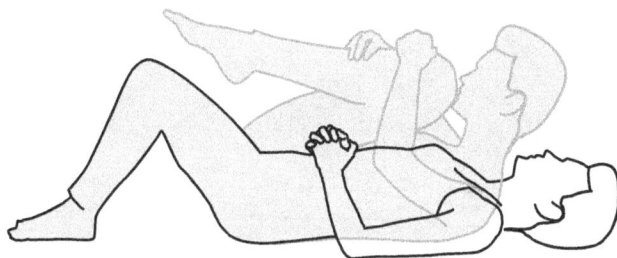

Knee to Chest Stretch

Bend your legs so that the soles of both feet are sitting flat on the bed. Now with both hands hold the underneath of your right thigh just above the knee. Slowly pull the knee towards your chest. Feel a gentle stretch right from your hamstrings through your big bum muscles into your back muscles. If you can, extend the stretch by raising your head towards the raised thigh. Repeat the same stretch with your left leg.

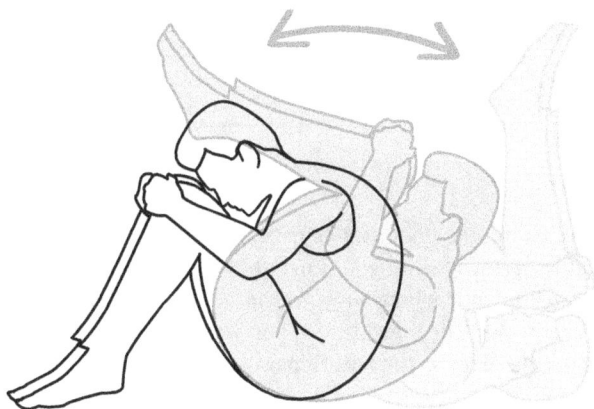

Rocking Motion

Now using both hands, grip both legs, lift as before and then start to gently rock your whole body backwards and forwards.

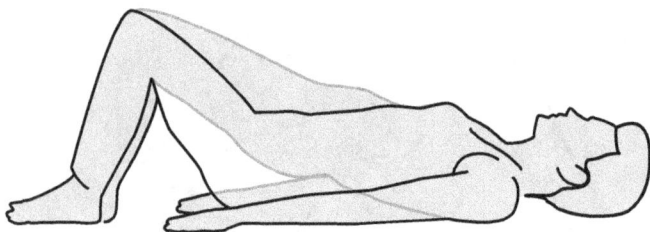

Pelvic Raise

With your feet still flat on the bed and with your knees bent, keep your feet and shoulders still. Raise your pelvis into the air, continue breathing in and out, hold for about 15 seconds and then slowly lower.

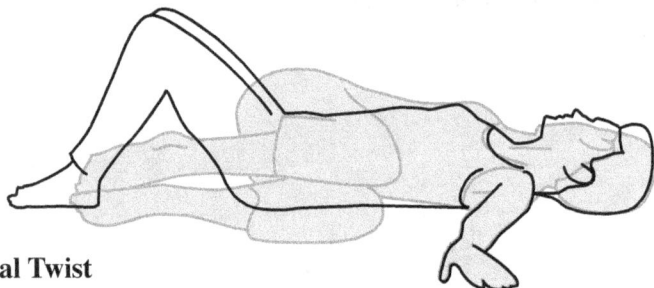

Spinal Twist

With your feet flat on the floor and your knees bent, stretch both arms out to each side and then slowly drop your knees to your left side. This will give you a twisting stretch to your whole body. At the same time turn your head in the opposite direction to the dropped legs. If you want to extend this stretch, move your top leg further over to the left. Repeat on your right side.

Clasped Hand Stretches

Slip off your footwear if you can. Standing, feet apart – about shoulder width. Knees slightly bent. Abdomen relaxed. Shoulders relaxed. Hands hanging gently by your sides. Breathe in and out gently two or three times just to help you relax.

Forwards

Clasp your hands together in front of you at waist height. Turn your clasped hands out in front and stretch your arms forward, drop your head forwards as you do it. Then return to your starting position. Allow the stretch to develop for about 20 seconds and feel the tension oozing out of your muscles.

Upwards

Slowly raise your hands in front of you in an arc out and then up so that they end up above your head. As you do this movement you will be turning your clenched hands outwards. At the same time you will be pulling your head back so you can see your clenched hands above you. Give yourself a nice slow gentle stretch by pushing your hands upwards. Develop for about 20 seconds.

Backwards

Then unclench your hands, move them out sideways and behind your back until they meet again. Clasp your hands once again when they meet. Now give yourself a nice slow gentle stretch by pushing your clenched hands back as you open out your chest. Once again, develop for about 20 seconds. Repeat the above sequence – if you wish.

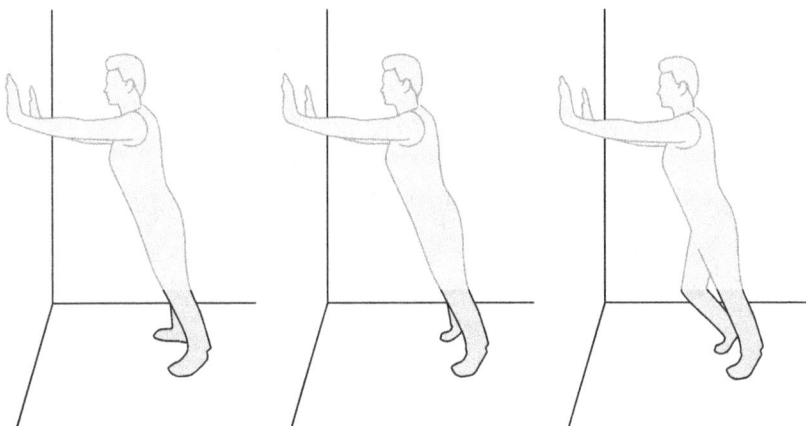

Lower Body Jiggle

Find a wall. Face the wall and place your two hands flat on the wall at shoulder height, fingers pointing up the wall. Now move both feet backwards a little so that you feel some of the weight of your body through your arms and hands. Your body is probably at an angle of about 45 degrees. Lift your heels up and stand on tiptoe. Now move from one foot to another by pushing each knee forward in turn. Do this a few times. Jiggle your body weight about as you do it and you will get to every part of your system. Feel all the tension escaping from your leg muscles and joints.

Limb Shaker

When you have finished give each leg a good shake in turn. Then shake each arm in turn. Then shake both hands at the same time. Shake away all that tension.

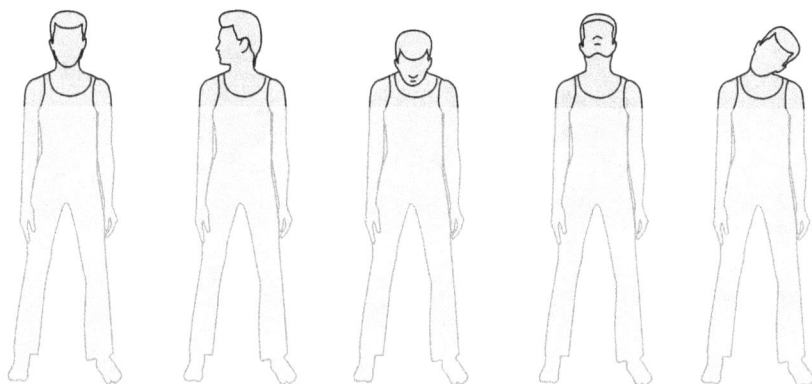

Neck Stretches
Stand or sit up straight, feet apart and arms by your sides.

To side
Slowly turn head to right and feel a gentle stretch. Don't force. Breathe in and out on turn. Keep your head upright and shoulders relaxed. Hold for 15 seconds. Repeat to left.

To front and back
Slowly drop your chin to your chest as you breathe in and out. Hold stretch for 15 seconds. Slowly raise your chin to the ceiling as you breathe in and out. Hold stretch for 15 seconds.

Head tilt
Slowly tilt your head to right so that your right ear approaches your shoulder as you breathe in and out. Hold stretch for 15 seconds. Repeat on left side.

STRENGTH EXERCISES

The Press Up

Though we all worry about our waistline modern life neglects our upper body – arms, shoulders and chest. That is a worry for good upper body strength that maintains good posture.

POSITION. Hands shoulder distance apart, palms flat with fingers pointing outwards. Look forward, keep your body straight – this works the core muscles – and your elbows tucked in at your sides. Exhale when pushing, inhale when you return.

Level 1 – Wall Push Off

Step back 2-3 feet from a wall. Place your hands against the wall at shoulder height. Lean into the wall, keeping your body straight and your arms extended. Your arms should be holding some of your weight. Now do the press up. Once you can do 10 move to the next level.

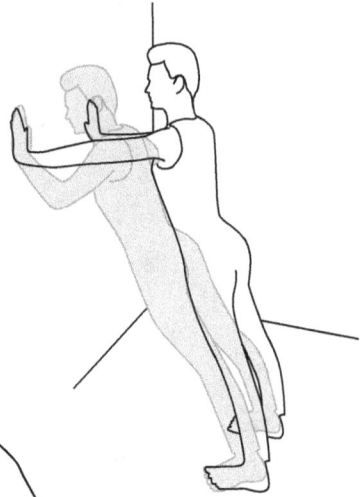

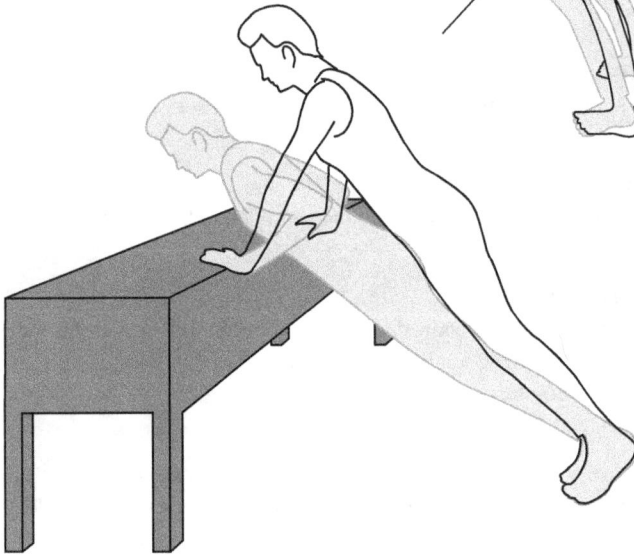

Level 2 – Waist High Push Off

Find a sturdy piece of furniture or ledge at about waist height. Take the push off position as described above. This time your weight is resting on your hands and balls of your feet. Aim for 10 reps and move on.

Level 3 – Knee-High Press Up

As above but using a bench, bed or sofa.

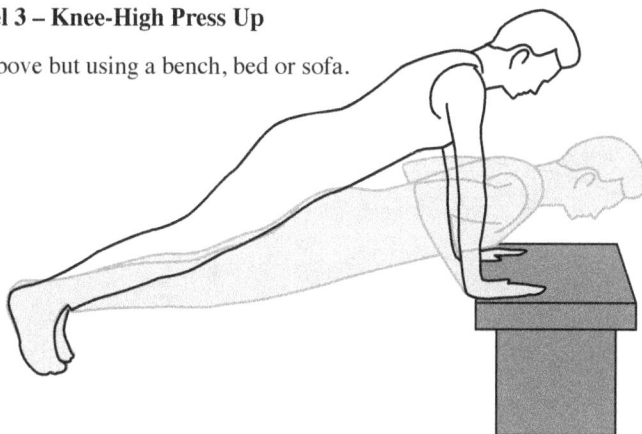

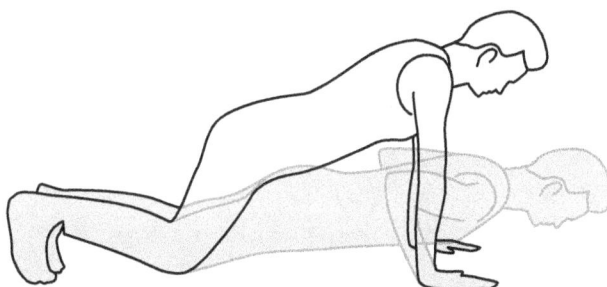

Level 4 – On Your Knees Press Up

This time you are on the floor and resting on your knees. Look slightly forward, and your upper body from your waist is now supported by your hands. Do the press up. You decide how far to lower your arms – do what is comfortable – no need to rush as it will improve as you build up your strength.

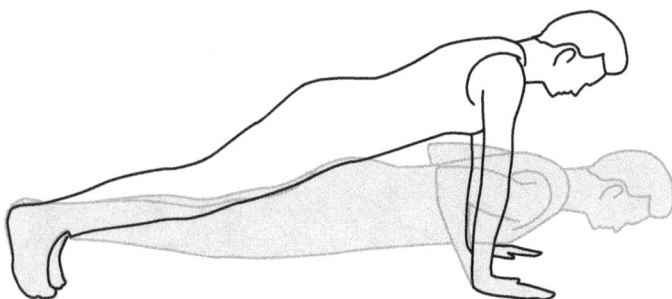

Level 5 – The Press Up

You are still on the floor. Look slightly forward, this time your body is suspended by your hands and the balls of your feet. Do the press up. You decide how far to lower your arms – do what is comfortable – no need to rush as it will improve as you build up your strength.

Leg Exercises

These will build stronger legs. Whatever you do, never let your knees bend more than 90 degrees.

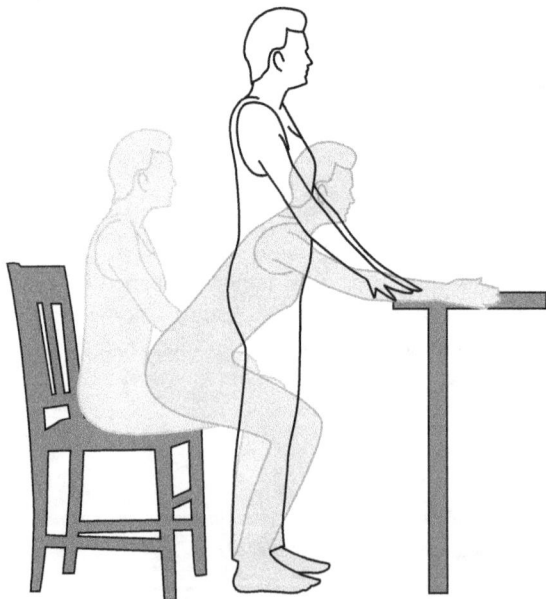

Level 1 – Find a chair high enough so that your knees do not bend more than 90 degrees when you sit. A dining chair is usually better than a modern comfy armchair. With a table to support you slowly lower yourself into the chair. Once there stand up again. Do not collapse into the chair, the slower the movement the harder your muscles work. The table is there for support but try and let the legs do the work. Once you can manage 10, move on to the next level.

Level 2 – This time complete the exercise without the table as support. Get to 10 then move on.

Level 3 – This time we are going to stand at the back of the chair and use that as support. This means that the legs are constantly working rather than having a rest between effort.

Level 4 – Now we are going to use no support. Stretch arms out in front to act as a balance.

Level 5 – Rather than return to standing when you straighten your leg, go up onto your toes.

Back Lift

The aim of the exercise is to strengthen the back muscles. Lie on the floor face down with your body in a straight line and your arms by your side. The position of the arms in this exercise makes the exercise progressively more difficult. Always lift the shoulders not just the head as you can strain the neck.

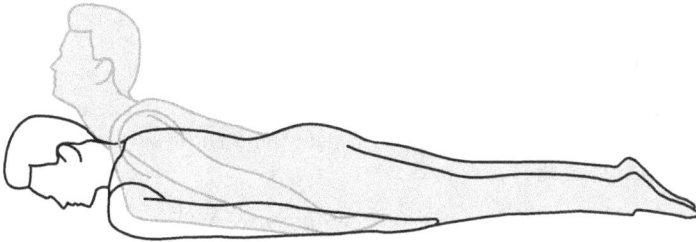

Level 1 – Lift your shoulders off the floor. Do not give up if you do not move. Your muscles are still working. As they strengthen you will move. Aim for an inch lift. Once you get to 10, move to the next level.

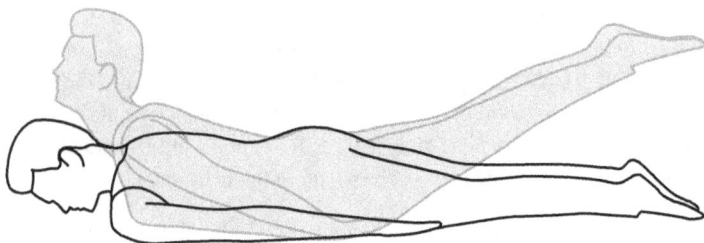

Level 2 – Now add your feet. Lift both an inch off the floor. Keep the arms at your side. This will actually restrict your movement and stop you getting carried away.

Level 3 – Place your hands on your head. And lift the shoulders only. Now the range of movement can increase.

Level 4 – Add the legs. This is a really challenging exercise but we all know how important strong backs are. Get to ten and move on.

Level 5 – Place the arms out in front of you. This increases dramatically the weight you are moving but the benefits are great.

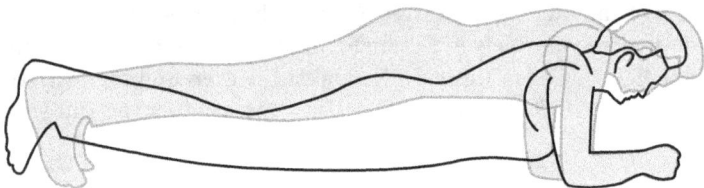

The Plank

Rather than traditional sit-ups that most ordinary folk struggle with we are going to use The Plank. It is a great way to build endurance in all your core muscles including the lower back.

Lie face down on the floor resting on your forearms, with your fists clenched flat on the floor. Push off the floor and rise onto your toes, as you continue to rest on your forearms. Aim to keep a straight line from your shoulders all the way down to your knees. Aim not to raise your hips or let your body sag. Try keeping your stomach, buttock and leg muscles tight during the workout. Remember – Keep breathing – DO NOT hold your breath. Hold the position for a few seconds or as long as is comfortable – don't strain.

There are no real levels in this; just aim to extend the number of seconds that you can hold, and the number of repetitions that you are able to do.

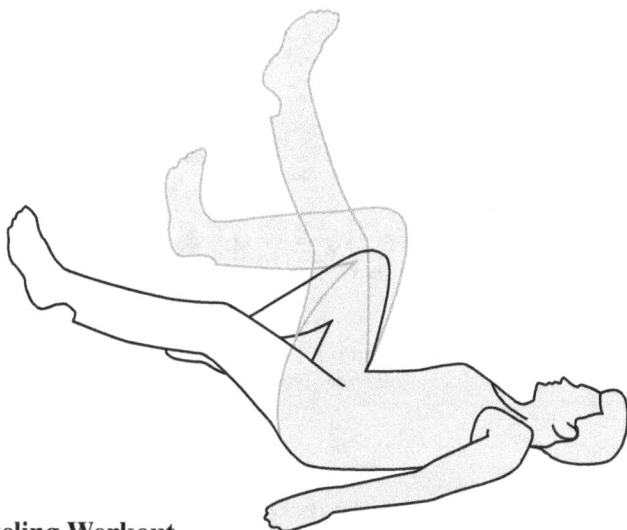

The Cycling Workout

Whilst you are on the floor, lie flat on your back. Press your lower back into the floor, and then raise your knees to about a 45-degree angle. Place your hands behind your head with your fingers interlaced. Rotate your legs as if you were cycling. Be careful not to twist or raise your back. Don't pull on your head or neck. Don't forget to breathe; don't hold your breath. Build up the number of leg movements gradually to about 60 to 70 pedals on each leg.

Chapter 32
Putting It All Together

'We are what we repeatedly do.
Excellence, therefore, is not an act but habit'.
Aristotle

Well done! You have reached the last but one chapter of the book.

So, how did you get here? At the beginning of the book we asked you to read Part I, the story part. Then we said you could carry on reading through Part II. This consists of the reasons why life can get you down and what you can do to become a Picture of Health.

Or you could browse through Part III before reading Part II. Part III is our 'Tool Box' of techniques and exercises. If you need a solution to a particular problem you will find it here. What did you do? There is no wrong way to do it – it's your book, and more importantly IT'S YOUR LIFE!

So how do we proceed in making your life a Picture of Health? Firstly, we are going to give you a little test. Nothing too difficult, and there are no wrong answers. This test will remind you of what was in the Tool Box and focus on what you need to improve in your life. After all, if you are a stressed-out athlete, you will probably need the mind focus tools more than the fitness tips.

Just a word of caution – all the Tools are interconnected. If you practice one tool, say the breathing tool, it will help you with the Mind Focus Tool later on. Similarly, if you stretch it will help you with building muscle in the Strength Tool.
And the more you practice them, the more they become a habit; the easier they will be to do and the benefits will be greater. Just as Aristotle said in the quote above.

So to the test. Read the description of the Tool on the right, and put a number from 1 to 5 on how important it is to you to master that tool. Remember, this is your test, no wrong answers. You can change your mind, rub things out, start again. Your choice. Your test, your life!

THE TOOL	PRIORITY
1. **Why Breathe? And How!** Using abdominal breathing to get more oxygen into your body and to relax. Abdominal breathing is the foundation of all the Tools here. It is simple to learn.	
2. **The Don't Panic Tool** This is your first priority. See page 193 'Which Tool First?'	1
3. **The Mind Focus Tool** Develop 'Real Relaxation' and learn how to grab a bit of calm wherever you are.	
4. **The Mind Power Tools** Unleash the power of your subconscious mind and use it to get what you want in your life.	
5. **The Writing Tools** Use the gift of writing to dump your past and present stresses – and plan for the future.	
6. **Inner Smile** Use the Power of Positive Affirmations to change the way you are and the way you see the world for the better.	
7. **Why Stretch? And How!** See how Flexibility is the King of Fitness and can stay with us forever.	
8. **The Bedstretcher Workout** Start the day Right with a mind and body work out whilst staying in bed!	
9. **AM/PM/Anytime Workout** Recharge your battery with a simple 5 minute work out.	
10. **Couch Potato Workout** Keep your six-pack flexible whilst relaxing.	
11. **The Strength Tool** How to pass the OOH-AAH Test! and build muscle for daily use.	
12. **The Walking Tool** The Best Exercise for aerobic conditioning.	
13. **The Food Tool** See page 193 'Adding the Food Tool'.	

Done that? Good. Now here is the plan. We are going to add a Tool a week to your life until you have mastered all of them. You have given a rough priority on how what you want to change in your life above. Use that as a guide to what you choose to do.

But before that we are going to show you how we are not going to proceed.

THE 14 WEEK GYM/SLIM CLUB WAY TO A NEW YOU

These clubs give you a rigid schedule to follow. You will lose X number of pounds a week. You will do so many sit-ups. In 14 weeks you will become what you want.

These clubs, books and regimes promise much but do they deliver? Well the simple answer is yes. If you are focused, determined and self-disciplined you will succeed.

But being focused, determined and self-disciplined seems a good place to be rather than a starting point to a new you!

What happens is we all start out with good intentions and then life gets in the way. We slip behind, get dejected and eventually give up. A failure.

THE PICTURE OF HEALTH CLUBS WAY TO A NEW YOU

Rather than life getting in the way, life is the way! We want you to make these tools part of you – a habit. And a good habit that you will do without thinking whilst enjoying your life.

The way the tools are designed is that one complements the other. You may struggle with one but when you pick up the next tool it will improve the one you struggle with. Each one builds on the other.

You cannot get despondent because there are no targets to reach only habits to acquire. And the great thing with habits is that once you have them they run automatically letting you focus on more important things, like enjoying life.

But first some rules:

1. Take time out to learn the tool. It is fairly impossible, for example, to learn the Bedstretcher exercise from a book, first thing in the morning. You will need to take time out to lie on a bed, pick up the book, read the exercise, put the book down, and do the exercise. Then moving on to the next exercise, pick up the book, read the exercise... Doing this will reap benefits later.

2. Remember that practice makes perfect. The more you do it the easier it will be to do and the more benefit you will gain from it.

3. Stick with a tool. Good habits take a while to form whilst bad habits seem to take twice as long to break. If you find a tool particularly difficult or of little benefit, remember that that tool will be enhanced by the next and the next tool will build in the one you struggle with.

4. If you really are failing with a tool after a week then let it rest for a few weeks until the other tools you use take hold and then try again. You will be surprised by the results when you re-try the tool again.

5. Alternate the tools you learn from high priority to low priority. This will give you breathing space so whilst you are concentrating on a low priority tool, you are internalising the higher one from last week.

WHICH TOOL FIRST?

The Tool we want you to try first is Tool 2, The 'Don't Panic!' Tool which gives yourself time to make a considered decision. Why? At only 2 pages long, and that includes the cut out panic card it is the shortest and yet the most important. It should take you about five minutes to learn. And that includes the time to find the scissors to cut out the card!

Wow! That was easy and you are now a week ahead.

Now consider which Tool you are going to learn next week. Do not map out the tools you will learn in advance. That calls for failure as you can slide behind. Rather, think of the next one at the end of the week. As your life changes and you become a Picture of Health your priorities will change.

ADDING THE FOOD TOOL

As we said in the food tool, we are going to give you some good eating habits to pick up. Like all good habits they take time to establish themselves. So be easy with yourself.

Here are the habits to pick up. Choose one a week to add to your new life. Whatever you choose is up to you.

IF YOU WANT TO GET THIN – CLEAR YOUR PLATE! Pick a plate that goes with your intended size and not your appetite – then clear it.

IF YOU WANT TO GET THIN – EAT MORE! Small light meals rather than one feast.

IF YOU WANT TO GET FIT – HALT YOUR DRINKING! Do not hit the bottle if you are Hungry, Alone, Lonely or Tired.

CUT OUT SUGAR – IT'S NOT COMPLICATED! Bin the processed carbohydrates.

GET THIN BY EATING YOUR GREENS – AND YOUR REDS, AND YOUR YELLOWS AND ORANGES. Get some colour on your plate.

GET THIN – EAT BREAKFAST. Crank up your metabolic rate.

IF YOU WANT TO GET THIN ON A DIET – CHEAT. Aim for a cheat and enjoy it rather than a load of little sins.

GET FIT – DRINK MORE get that water down you.

BE A GOOD PERSON AND OBEY THE CURFEW
Obey the Caffeine Curfew.
Obey the Carbohydrate Curfew.

YOUR MOST IMPORTANT TARGET IN THE WEEKS AHEAD

It is your life and we want you to take control of it and enjoy it. That is your most important goal. Anything else, weight loss, stress reduction, relaxation – they all come second to this most important target.

- **How you proceed is up to you.**
- **We prefer the Less is More approach – easing yourself into life-changing habits.**
- **If you are a goal-orientated person then set them – be rigid. Draw tables. Do what you feel to get there.**
- **But if you fail, do not be hard on yourself.**
- **We all fall down at times.**
- **What matters is not that we fall, but that we get up and try again.**
- **Take the first steps to a new Picture of Health Clubs life.**

Chapter 33
And Finally...

'This is not the end. It is not even the beginning of the end.
But it is, perhaps, the end of the beginning'.
Winston Churchill 10 Nov. 1942

Everything in our book is designed to be easy to learn, easy to do and easy to include into your lifestyle, no matter how busy you may be.

- It will dramatically improve the quality of your life.
- Can you afford to ignore it?
- This book can be the beginning of your new improved lifestyle.
- If you have accepted the challenge then this book is the end of your beginning.
- You are now on a path whose ultimate end is to be a 'Picture of Health'.

Follow us on:

Please visit our website at www.pictureofhealthclubs.com AND sign up for our FREE regular blogs and newsletters.

Unwind body and mind...

www.ingramcontent.com/pod-product-compliance
Lightning Source LLC
LaVergne TN
LVHW051518080426
835509LV00017B/2100